How To Do Your Own Small Business Bookkeeping

Utilizing QuickBooks Simple Start 2010 Free Version

A Hands-On, Step-by-Step Guide for Entrepreneurs and Virtual Assistants

by Lily E. Chambers
Certified Professional Secretary
Certified QuickBooks User

First printing: July 2011

ISBN-13: 978-0-9788782-7-6
ISBN-10: 0-9788782-7-2

Library of Congress Control Number: 2011929487

Graphico Publishing
a subsidiary of 50 State Notary
1601 West Fifth Avenue, Suite 123
Columbus, Ohio 43212-2303
Phone: 614.801-9977
Email: victoria@graphicopublishing.com
Internet: http://www.graphicopublishing.com

How To Do Your Own Small Business Bookkeeping

Utilizing QuickBooks Simple Start 2010 Free Version

A Hands-On, Step-by-Step Guide for Entrepreneurs and Virtual Assistants

by Lily E. Chambers
Certified Professional Secretary
Certified QuickBooks User

THE VIRTUAL OFFICE GODDESS, LLC
Bookkeeping & Office Support Services
http://www.virtualofficegoddess.com

Introduction

This book was taught as an online class and has retained the class format; it will teach you basic bookkeeping skills for your business. Although it is not necessary for proper utilization of the QuickBooks Simple Start program, I highly recommend that you complete the research project and final exam as this information will not only be useful to you in the future, but the final exam will also help reinforce what you have learned.

This book covers accounting terminology, how to set up and maintain your bookkeeping system, and year-end archiving. This book WILL NOT prepare you for setting up and/or maintaining other business' accounting. I advise you to verify your chart of accounts with a CPA prior to beginning your data entry.

This book consists of four lessons with a research project following the first lesson and a final exam at the end. The book contains the following chapters:

Chapter 1: Basic accounting terminology & information (Lesson 1)
Chapter 2: Research Project
Chapter 3: Basic bookkeeping and accounting records set up (Lesson 2)
Chapter 4: Maintenance of your bookkeeping records (Lesson 3)
Chapter 5: Year-end Procedures Lesson 4)
Chapter 6: Final Exam
Chapter 7: Answers to the Research Project and Final Exam

QuickBooks Simple Start (free edition) can be downloaded at:

http://quickbooks.intuit.com/qb/products/common/direct_download/email.jsp

Table of Contents

Chapter 1

Bookkeeping Basics

Section One: Accounting Terminology

Many people hear the words "accounting" or "bookkeeping" and immediately panic. Although these words strike fear into many hearts, they are a necessary part of being a business owner. The best way to reduce or eliminate fear is to face it head on. Oftentimes, fear results from ignorance of the subject, not from the subject itself. Therefore, we will begin by acquainting you with some of the basic terms used in accounting – the ones you are most likely to need to understand.

Debit & Credit – these two terms can be very confusing, with good reason. When you speak to your banker, a "credit" means you are *increasing* your account balance and a "debit" means you are *decreasing* your account balance. However, in accounting, these terms often mean the exact opposite! For example, when you make a deposit into your bank account in your accounting records, you will record a "debit" to your bank account and a "credit" to income received. Debit and credit entries must always match, or be in "balance." We'll go into where to record "debits" and "credits" later in the book.

How Debits and Credits Get Posted

Account	**Debit**	**Credit**
Assets	Increases	Decreases
Liabilities	Decreases	Increases
Income	Decreases	Increases
Expenses	Increases	Decreases

Accounts Receivable (A/R) – money *owed to your company* for providing services or products. Once the money is received, it becomes "income."

Accounts Payable (A/P) – money *owed by your company to vendors* for services or products you received. Once the money is paid, it becomes an "expense." A vendor can be a direct supplier, such as your phone company, or an indirect supplier, such as your credit card company;

anyone to whom you owe money that will be paid promptly.

Income – money received that your company has earned. This can be from providing services to clients, or selling products (see definition for A/R).

Expense – money that your company has paid out for services or products (see definition for A/P).

Net Income – the money remaining after subtracting expenses from income. A "Profit" is a positive balance and a "Loss" is a negative balance.

Asset – items of value *owned by your company,* i.e. purchased by your company or in your company's name. Example, computer equipment or office furniture purchased with company funds or in the company's name, company bank accounts, etc. Accounts Receivable are also considered an asset because, as pending income, they are considered to be valuable; the equivalent of the money in your bank account.

Liability – debts owed by your company. This includes outstanding vendor invoices, bank loans, etc. Short-term liabilities are debts that will be paid during the current fiscal year. Long-term liabilities are debts that will be paid over the course of more than one accounting period (a 2-year bank loan would be considered a long-term liability).

Owners Equity – the amount of money you invest into your company. This will be recorded as a General Journal entry. Debit = checking (or account in which you invested money) and Credit = Owner's Equity account.

Owner's Draw – the money that you withdraw from your company for personal use. This can be recorded as a General Journal entry. Debit = owner's draw and Credit = checking or other account from which you withdrew funds for personal use (e.g., federal tax deposits). Personal purchases *should not* be made through the company but rather a check should be issued by the company to you personally.

Accrual Basis - accrual basis reports count sales as of the invoice date and count expenses as of the date the goods or services were received.

Cash Basis - cash basis reports show actual 'real-time' cash inflow and outflow.

Chart of Accounts – a listing of your asset, liability, income, expense, bank accounts, etc. This account listing is normally placed in the same order as you will see on your financial statements.

Retained Earnings – profits that are left with the company after the end of the fiscal year.

Fiscal Year – same as a "financial year" or "financial accounting period" (usually January 1 to December 31).

Section Two: Budget

This is another area where people start to panic. BUT – a well thought out budget can make a big difference in running a successful business. If you don't have the money to buy office supplies, pay for your website or phone line, marketing, etc. your business won't last long, will it? Thus, the need to create a budget. A budget is important to help you keep track of whether or not your business is making a profit. (The definition of a 'successful' business and necessary if you wish to make a living from it!) A budget doesn't have to be a big complicated structure, simply a straight-forward list of (anticipated) income and expenses. A budget should be an "organic" or "living" document, meaning that it can, and should, be modified on a regular basis to reflect your current financial status. We will discuss how to create a budget in Chapter 3.

Section Three: Taxes

They say the only certainties in life are death and taxes. Well, everyone wants their share of the taxes – fair or not!

Federal Requirements

Estimated Tax Deposits are due to the federal government on April 15, July 15, September 15, and January 15. Estimated Tax Deposits are required for both income and self-employment (Social Security/Medicare) tax. Corporate annual tax returns are due to be filed on March 15. All other annual tax returns are due to be filed on April 15.

Sole proprietorships, partnerships, and LLCs are not considered separate from their owners for tax purposes. Partnerships and LLCs are what the IRS call a "pass-through entity." This means that business income passes through the business to the Partners or LLC members, who report their share of profits -- or losses -- on their individual income tax returns. Sole Proprietors and each Partner or LLC member must make quarterly estimated tax payments to the IRS.

While Partnerships and LLCs don't pay taxes, both Partnerships and co-owned LLCs must file Form 1065, an informational return, with the IRS each year. This form sets out each Partner's or LLC member's share of the businesses profits (or losses), which the IRS reviews to make sure Partners and LLC members are correctly reporting their income.

State Requirements

Each State has different requirements. You will need to find the requirements and filing deadlines for your State from their Department of Revenue website.

Employee Taxes

When you are starting out, you will most likely not have any employees (sole proprietors and LLC principals are not considered employees). However, if you eventually hire employees, you should be aware that employers must withhold Federal withholding, State withholding, Social Security Tax, and Medicare Tax from employee pay. In addition, the employer matches the SSI and Medicare deductions. These deductions are deposited to the IRS on a quarterly basis (unless the IRS instructs otherwise) through the E.F.T.P.S. system using Form 941 (Employer's Quarterly Federal Tax Return). The employer is also responsible for Federal Unemployment (Form 940) and State Unemployment payments.

Completing a W-9

You may receive a W-9 Form from some of your clients requesting your Federal Tax ID Number (EIN/TIN). They will use this information to send you a 1099 Form at the end of the year (See Chapter 5--Section One). Complete the section marked with the lighter (red) arrows and fill in EITHER your Social Security Number OR the Federal Tax ID Number (Employer ID Number) you were issued (preferably the EIN/TIN). Sign and date the form and send it back to the requestor (their information should be in the section marked with a darker (blue) arrow) for their records.

Form **W-9**
(Rev. October 2007)
Department of the Treasury
Internal Revenue Service

Request for Taxpayer Identification Number and Certification

Give form to the requester. Do not send to the IRS.

Print or type
Specific Instructions on page 2

Name (as shown on your income tax return)

Business name, if different from above

Check appropriate box: ☐ Individual/Sole proprietor ☐ Corporation ☐ Partnership
☐ Limited liability company. Enter the tax classification (D=disregarded entity, C=corporation, P=partnership) ▶
☐ Other (see instructions) ▶

☐ Exempt payee

Address (number, street, and apt. or suite no.)

Requester's name and address (optional)

City, state, and ZIP code

List account number(s) here (optional)

Part I **Taxpayer Identification Number (TIN)**

Enter your TIN in the appropriate box. The TIN provided must match the name given on Line 1 to avoid backup withholding. For individuals, this is your social security number (SSN). However, for a resident alien, sole proprietor, or disregarded entity, see the Part I instructions on page 3. For other entities, it is your employer identification number (EIN). If you do not have a number, see *How to get a TIN* on page 3.

Social security number

or

Employer identification number

Note. If the account is in more than one name, see the chart on page 4 for guidelines on whose number to enter.

Part II **Certification**

Under penalties of perjury, I certify that:

1. The number shown on this form is my correct taxpayer identification number (or I am waiting for a number to be issued to me), and
2. I am not subject to backup withholding because: (a) I am exempt from backup withholding, or (b) I have not been notified by the Internal Revenue Service (IRS) that I am subject to backup withholding as a result of a failure to report all interest or dividends, or (c) the IRS has notified me that I am no longer subject to backup withholding, and
3. I am a U.S. citizen or other U.S. person (defined below).

Certification instructions. You must cross out item 2 above if you have been notified by the IRS that you are currently subject to backup withholding because you have failed to report all interest and dividends on your tax return. For real estate transactions, item 2 does not apply. For mortgage interest paid, acquisition or abandonment of secured property, cancellation of debt, contributions to an individual retirement arrangement (IRA), and generally, payments other than interest and dividends, you are not required to sign the Certification, but you must provide your correct TIN. See the instructions on page 4.

Sign Here **Signature of U.S. person** ▶ **Date** ▶

Section Four: Useful Websites

IRS *Website* -

The IRS website (www.irs.gov) can be a great resource. On it you will find Federal tax deposit requirements, a Tax Deadline Calendar, and W-9 forms among other valuable information. Their "Small Business and Self-Employed One-Stop Resource" website (http://www.irs.gov/businesses/small/) is well worth checking out.

Your State *Department* of Revenue Website -

You will use your State Department of Revenue website to determine tax filing deadlines for your State. Many states have useful information for small businesses both on their Revenue Department and Secretary of State websites.

My State's websites (record here for future reference)

State Revenue Department: ____________________

Secretary of State: ____________________________

Small Business Administration Website -
The small business Administration website is located at http://www.sba.gov/ and is an excellent resource for small businesses, whether just starting out or well-established.

Section Five: Commonly Used Reports

To answer this question...	Use this report
How much money did my company make or lose over a specific period of time?	Profit & Loss Standard (In Company & Financial)
Which invoices or statement charges haven't been paid and when are they due?	A/R Aging Detail (In Customers & Receivables)
How much does my company owe each vendor and are any payments overdue?	A/P Aging Detail (In Vendors & Payables)
What is the value of my company (its assets, liabilities, and equity), and where can I see the total balance for each type of account?	Balance Sheet Summary (In Company & Financial)
What is the recent activity in all my company's accounts, with beginning and ending balances for each account?	General Ledger (In Accountant & Taxes)
What are the total sales for each customer and job?	Sales by Customer Summary (In Sales)
Which items and/or services bring in the most/least income?	Sales by Item Summary (In Sales)
What are my company's total expenses for each vendor?	Expenses by Vendor Summary (In Company & Financial)
Where is the information I need for my federal income tax forms?	Income Tax Summary Income Tax Detail (In Accountant & Taxes)
For my company's total sales, how much is taxable, at what rate, and how much sales tax is currently due to be paid?	Sales Tax Liability (In Vendors & Payables)

Chapter 2

Research Project

RESEARCH PROJECT

IRS Website (www.irs.gov)

1. What ID number should you use for your business in place of your Social Security number?	
2. What publication number is the "A Virtual Small Business Tax Workshop" DVD?	
3. What publication number is the "Tax Calendar for Small Businesses and Self-employed?"	
4. What is the definition of "Burden of Proof"	
5. How long should you keep your tax records under normal circumstances?	
6. "To be deductible, a business expense must be both ordinary and necessary." a) What is the definition of an 'ordinary' expense? b) What is the definition of a 'necessary' expense?	
7. What types of expenses can you deduct for the 'business use of your home?'	

Your State Revenue Department website

1. What is the address of your State Revenue Dept. website?	
2. Does your State require Estimated Self-employment Tax Deposits? a) When are they due? b) How much is required?	
3. Does your State offer on-line tax classes?	
4. Does your State offer an on-line tax calendar?	

Chapter 3

Bookkeeping and Accounting Records Setup

Section One: Time Tracking

One of the first things you want to have in place is some type of time tracking process. Many entrepreneurs find a physical timesheet to be much more practical than an electronic time tracking system (although, of course, what you use to track your time is a personal preference). Tracking your time will help you to see where your time is being spent. You may find that the "15 minute project" actually took you 30 or more minutes, whether because you miscalculated the time or because of interruptions.

You also may find that you are spending considerably more time than you had realized on client phone calls/ IMs/ emails, etc. Your timesheet information will assist you in billing your clients, calculating future project time estimates, and to estimate income, which you will need to help you properly set up a budget; a budget is critical for any properly run business.

EXAMPLE OF TIME TRACKING WORKSHEET (Excel)

Time Period: 08/01-08/31/..

Date:	Client Name	Time In:	Break time:	Time Out:	Total Time:	Description
8/1/20..	Admin	7:45 AM		8:00 AM	0.25	check email
8/1/20..	PIC	8:00 AM		8:10 AM	0.17	t/c client re: new cc to pay
8/1/20..	Admin	8:10 AM		8:30 AM	0.33	pay bills
8/1/20..	Admin	5:00 PM		5:45 PM	0.75	Make bank deposit/ backup files to safe dep box hard drive
8/1/20..	Admin	6:45 PM		7:00 PM	0.25	open mail/ enter bills in QB
8/1/20..	Yoga	7:00 PM		7:15 PM	0.25	t/c re: receipts not rcvd in mail
8/1/20..	PIC	7:15 PM		8:45 PM	1.5	sort/enter July receipts
8/1/20..	Aromatics	8:45 PM		10:30 PM	1.75	sort/enter July receipts
					0	
					0	
					0	
	TOTAL TIME:	5.25				

Client	Total for Type	Expenses	
Aromatics	1.75		
PIC	1.67		
Yoga	0.25		
Character	0		
Standard	0		
Cooper	0		
	0		
Admin	1.58		

You should track your administrative time as well as the client billable time. This reminds you to keep your non-billable hours as low as possible and again, helps you with your budget. The actual time and total time on this example sheet are calculated by Excel.

Section Two: Creating A Budget

As stated above, a budget is critical for any properly run business. Start by making a list of all of the expenses you know you have to cover: website, phone line, insurance, etc. Next you need to estimate your income for each month. Your timesheet can help you to estimate how much your income will be based on the client time that you have already earned. If you do not have timesheets to go by, you can estimate how much income you will need based on your expenses.

Once you have these numbers you can begin to build a basic budget. The Excel spreadsheet that you use for your budget can also be used to track when your bills are due and paid, when your estimated tax payments are due, how much you need to deposit for your estimated taxes, and a reminder to reconcile your bank/credit card accounts. An example of a budget spreadsheet is below.

EXAMPLE OF ANNUAL BUDGET & BILL TRACKING WORKSHEET (Excel)

DEADLINES CALENDAR

Due	$	Name	JAN	FEB	MAR	APR	MAY	JUN	JUL	AUG	SEP	OCT	NOV	DEC	
1	[illegible]	Liability Insurance		225											
1	[illegible]	E&O Insurance		385											
1	[illegible]	Surety Bond			100										
12	[illegible]	Professional Membership		60											
13	[illegible]	Website - Annual							60						
18	[illegible]	Phone/ Internet Service	90	90	90	90	90	90	90	90	90	90	90	90	
30	[illegible]	Domain - Annual						38							
30	[illegible]	PO Box - 6 mo	22					22							
30	[illegible]	Secretary of State Annual Filing								10					
		Monthly Bill Total	112	535	190	90	90	150	150	100	90	90	90	90	Estimated Net Annual Income
		Estimated Income	7,200	7,200	7,200	7,200	7,200	7,200	7,200	7,200	7,200	7,200	3,600	3,600	
		Difference (profit)	7,088	6,665	7,010	7,110	7,110	7,050	7,050	7,100	7,110	7,110	3,510	3,510	$ 77,423
		Miscellaneous (Ofc Sply, Printing,etc.)													
		Marketing (10% of profit)	709	667	701	711	711	705	705	710	711	711	351	351	
		Equip, software, etc. (10% of profit)	709	667	701	711	711	705	705	710	711	711	351	351	Est. Annual Tax Liability
		Fed. Est. Income Tax (18%)	1,276	1,200	1,262	1,280	1,280	1,269	1,269	1,278	1,280	1,280	632	633	$ 13,836 14
		Fed. Est. Self-employment Tax (15.3%)	975	975	975	975	975	975	975	975	975	975	975	975	$ 11,694 07
		State Est. Income Tax (7%)	496	467	491	498	498	494	494	497	498	498	246	246	$ 5,419.81
		Total to deposit in Savings	4,164	3,974	4,129	4,174	4,174	4,147	4,147	4,170	4,174	4,174	2,554	2,554	$ 31,049.82
		EXPECTED MONTHLY INCOME AFTER EXPENSES	2,924	2,691	2,881	2,936	2,936	2,903	2,903	2,930	2,936	2,936	956	956	Est Net Income After Taxe
															$ 46,373.18
		RECONCILIATIONS (X WHEN DONE)													
		Bank Checking Reconcilation Done?	X	X	X										
		Bank Savings Reconciliation Done?	X	X	X										
		Credit Card Reconciliation Done?	X	X	X										
		Petty Cash Reconciliation Done?	X	X	X										
		FILING DEADLINES (X WHEN PAID/FILED)													
15		Estimated Federal wholding tax due	X			$ 3,484		$ 3,484			$ 3,484				
28		1099 to IRS		X											
30		1099 to vendor/subcontractor	X												

The bills are listed by their due date. The second column is the annual or monthly amount of the bill. The darker (blue) square indicates when the bill is actually due lighter squares are calculated totals). When each bill is paid, change the color of the numbers to light gray. This is an immediate indication that the bill has been paid and a red flag if it has not and is due shortly.

Marketing, equipment/software, and estimated tax deposit funds go into a savings account until they are needed; at that time, the necessary funds are transferred back into the checking account. At the end of each month, change the estimated income amount to the actual amount of income received that month, therefore making the "estimated tax deposits due" more accurate. By combining the budget and bill tracking spreadsheet, you quickly have your information available at your fingertips.

The reconciliation section is a reminder to reconcile your bank accounts, credit card accounts, loan accounts, and petty cash in QuickBooks. The filing deadlines section keeps you on track of when and how much estimated tax to deposit and a reminder to issue required end-of-year tax forms to your vendors.

Part of the year-end process, which we will cover later in the book, is to set up the budget for the following year based on the prior year's actual expenses. There are multiple tabs in the spreadsheet. The first one is the original budget sheet that is used as a template to create new tabs for each year; you should keep the previous year's tabs for historical reference.

Section Three: Setting Up QuickBooks Simple Start

Now you are ready to set up your QuickBooks Simple Start company file. Hopefully, you have already downloaded and installed the QuickBooks Simple Start program on your computer (http://quickbooks.intuit.com/product/accounting-software/free-accounting-software.jsp.) If you have not installed the program, now is the time to do so.

When you install your QuickBooks Simple Start be sure and leave "Open QuickBooks" **checked** and **uncheck** "Help me get started." Once the installation is completed and QuickBooks Simple Start opens, you should see a screen that looks like this:

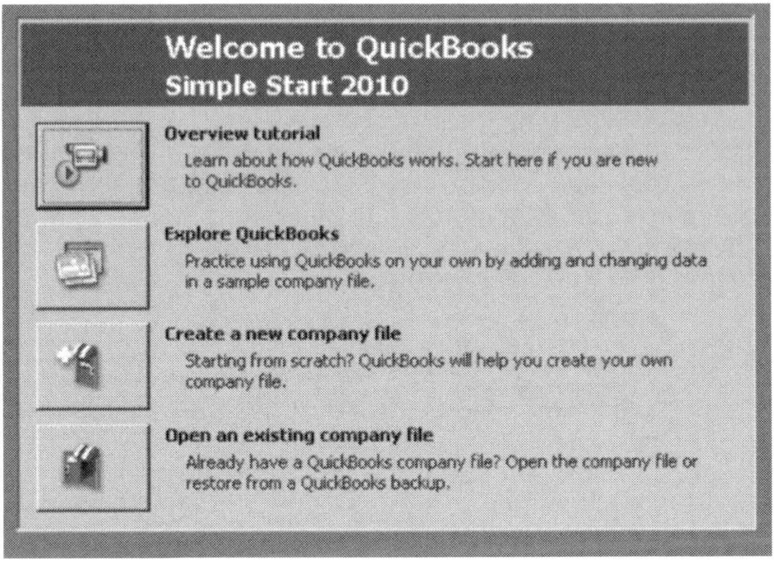

You are certainly welcome to go through the tutorial or explore QuickBooks, but for our purposes click on "Create a new company file." (To start the "Create a new company file wizard", click on file--new company on the top left corner of your menu bar.) When you click on "Create a new company file" the Simple Start Setup wizard will take you through the following questions (use the table below to fill in the answers if you wish prior to setting up your file):

Company name	
Company address	
City, State, Zip	
Company phone #	
Company fax #	
Company email	
Company website	
How is your company organized? Sole Proprietorship (it has one owner) using Tax Form 1040 Partnership or Limited Liability Company (it has two or more owners) using Tax Form 1065 S Corporation (is a small business with one or more shareholders) using Fax Form 1120S Corporation (it is a large business with one or more shareholders) using Tax Form 1120 Non-profit organization (it does not pay taxes) using Tax Form 990 Other/None	
When do your customers pay you for the products and services you sell? My customers pay me at the time of the sale I send my customers a bill and receive payment later Both (default)	
Do you create estimates for any of your customers?	
Do you charge sales tax when you make a sale?	

Once you complete the new company set up wizard and enter a company name, QuickBooks Simple Start will create your company file and you will see this screen:

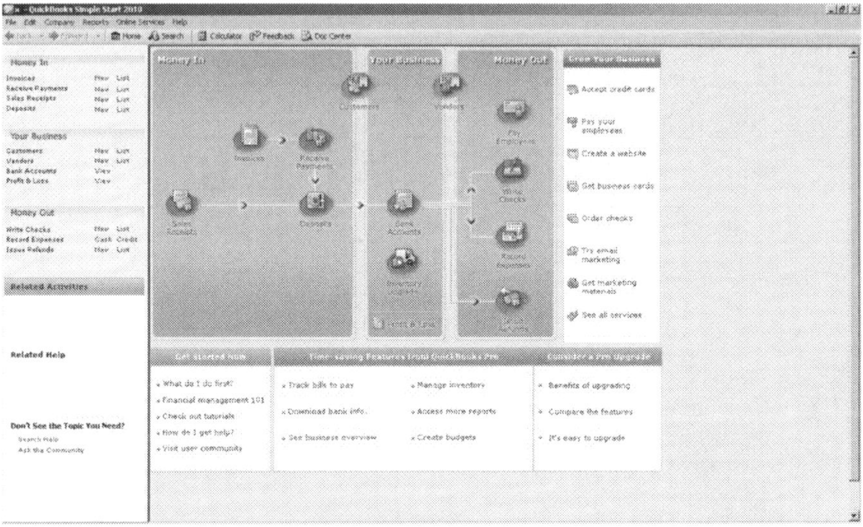

Section Four: Setting Up a Chart of Accounts in QuickBooks Simple Start

QuickBooks Simple Start has set up a basic Chart of Accounts based on your answer to "how is your company organized." To find your default Chart of Accounts, either press CTRL-A or go to Company--lists--chart of accounts.

Let's look at the most common types of Chart of Accounts set up by QuickBooks Simple Start:

Sole Proprietor Chart of Accounts

Name
◆Payroll Liabilities
◆Opening Balance Equity
◆Owner's Capital
◆Retained Earnings
◆Discounts Given
◆Sales
◆Advertising
◆Car and Truck Expenses
◆Commissions and fees
◆Contract labor
◆Employee benefit programs
◆Insurance (other than health)
◆Interest (other than mortgage)
◆Legal and professional fees
◆Meals and Entertainment
◆Mortgage interest
◆Office expenses
◆Payroll Expenses
◆Postage and Delivery
◆Rent of other business property
◆Rent of vehicles or equipment
◆Repairs and maintenance
◆Supplies
◆Taxes and licenses
◆Travel
◆Utilities
◆Other Income
◆Other Expenses

Partnership or LLC Chart of Accounts

Name
◆Payroll Liabilities
◆Opening Balance Equity
◆Partner One Equity
◆Partner Two Equity
◆Retained Earnings
◆Discounts Given
◆Sales
◆Advertising and Promotions
◆Automobile Expense
◆Bank Service Charges
◆Depreciation Expense
◆Dues and Subscriptions
◆Insurance
◆Legal and Professional Fees
◆Licenses and Permits
◆Meals and Entertainment
◆Payroll Expenses
◆Postage and Delivery
◆Printing and Reproduction
◆Rent
◆Repairs and Maintenance
◆Supplies and Materials
◆Telephone
◆Travel
◆Utilities
◆Interest Income
◆Other Miscellaneous Income
◆Other Expenses

There are a few necessary differences based on the type of organization you chose for your company (such as Owner's Capital vs. Partner One Equity), but for the most part, the charts are very close. Some of the accounts are unnecessary and should be deleted or inactivated to reduce confusion (i.e. Payroll Liabilities won't be needed unless you have employees). Some accounts will need to be renamed, most of them need their tax-line mapping changed, you will need to create some new accounts, and you may wish to create multiple similar accounts to better track your expenses (e.g., Insurance - liability, Insurance – E&O, etc.).

Here are the accounts I recommend you use to start:

ACCOUNT NAME	ACCOUNT TYPE
Accounts Receivable	Accounts Receivable
Cash on Hand	Other Current Asset
Undeposited Funds	Other Current Asset
Income Summary	Equity
Opening Balance Equity	Equity
Owner's Equity (LLC & Sole Proprietor) OR [Partner One Name] Equity / [Partner Two Name] Equity (Partnership – make and equity account for each partner)	Equity
Owner's Draw (LLC & Sole Proprietor)	Equity
Services (changed from Sales)	Income
Bank service charges	Expense
Dues and subscriptions	Expense
Insurance – [type] (i.e. Liability, E&O, etc. Use multiple accounts for multiple insurance types)	Expense
Interest	Expense
Legal and professional Fees	Expense
Licenses and Permits	Expense
Marketing	Expense
Meals and entertainment	Expense
Postage and delivery	Expense
Printing and reproduction	Expense
Professional development	Expense
Repairs and maintenance	Expense
Supplies and materials	Expense
Telephone and internet (change from telephone)	Expense
Travel – mileage (changed from travel)	Expense
Website and domain	Expense
Client Retainer (IF you accept pre-payment of funds)	Other current liability

Note that there are no miscellaneous accounts. All items should be assigned to a specific account. *I recommend you verify your chart of accounts with your accountant BEFORE starting data entry*; this is the setup my accountant approved for my bookkeeping business and your accountant may suggest some different accounts. This setup will, however, get you started on setting up your books.

QuickBooks Simple Start defaults the tax-line mapping of most of the accounts to "Other deduction: other." You may wish to edit your accounts to match the tax-line mapping column that best represents the account name. To edit, delete or inactivate an account, right-click on the account name to bring up the menu options. This menu will also allow you to add new accounts.

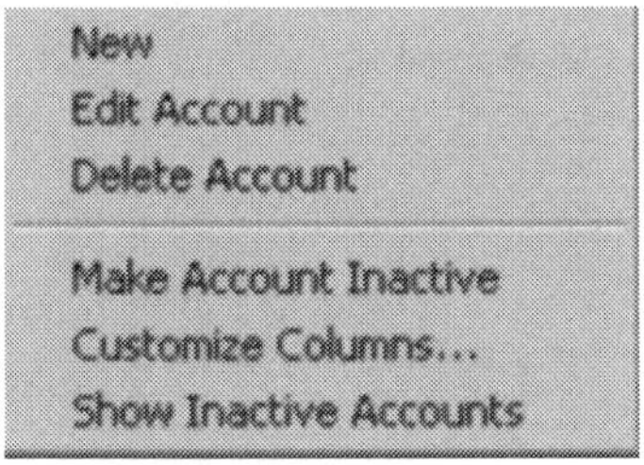

When you add a new account, you will need to also add the tax-line mapping. To add a new account, right click in the Chart of Accounts list and choose "New." You will see this screen:

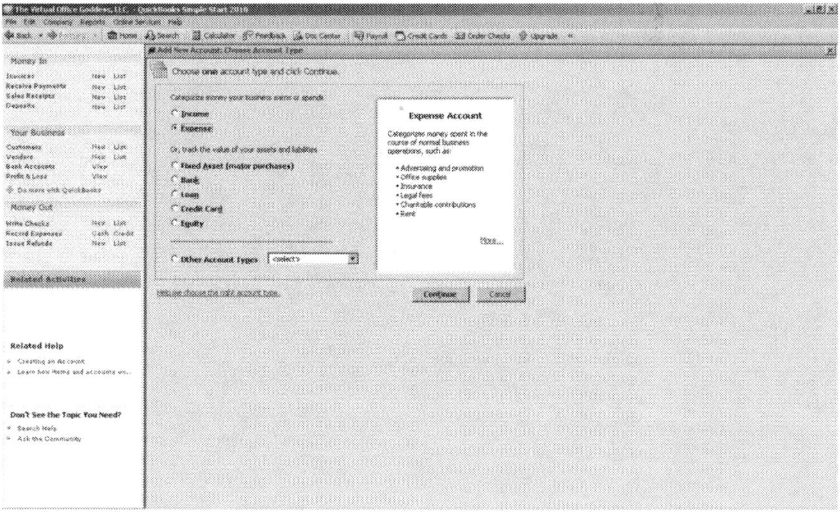

Most of the accounts that you set up will be expense accounts. Click on "Expense" then click "Continue." The next screen you see will be this one:

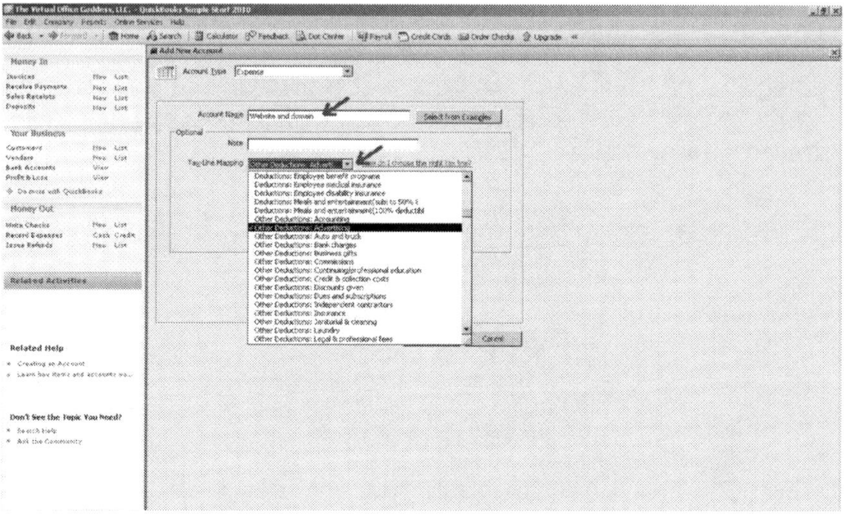

Enter the new account name, click on the drop down list, and choose an appropriate tax-line mapping item. When you click on "Save & Close" your new item will be in the Chart of Accounts.

Section Five: Setting Up Bank Account(s)/Credit Card Accounts

Now that your basic Chart of Accounts is set up, you need to add your bank and credit card accounts to the list. This is the same process as adding a new expense account except, of course, you will click on "Bank" or "Credit Card" instead of "Expense." When you click on "Continue", you will see the 'Add New Account' screen.

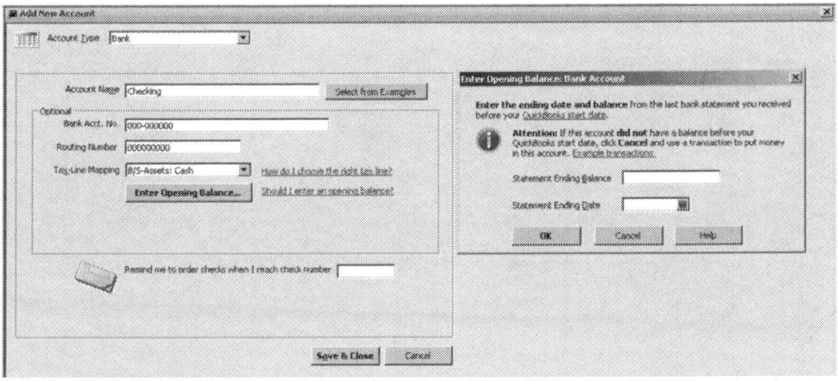

After entering the account name (e.g. Checking), click on "Enter Opening Balance" and fill in the statement ending balance and statement ending date from the last statement you received in December of the previous year. If the bank account was opened during the current year enter a statement ending balance of zero.

Once you are finished entering your bank checking and savings accounts, repeat the process with your credit card accounts. After entering the account name (e.g. Local Bank MasterCard) and account number, click on "Enter Opening Balance" and fill in the statement ending balance and statement ending date from the last statement you received in December of the previous year. If the credit card account was opened during the current year enter a statement ending balance of zero.

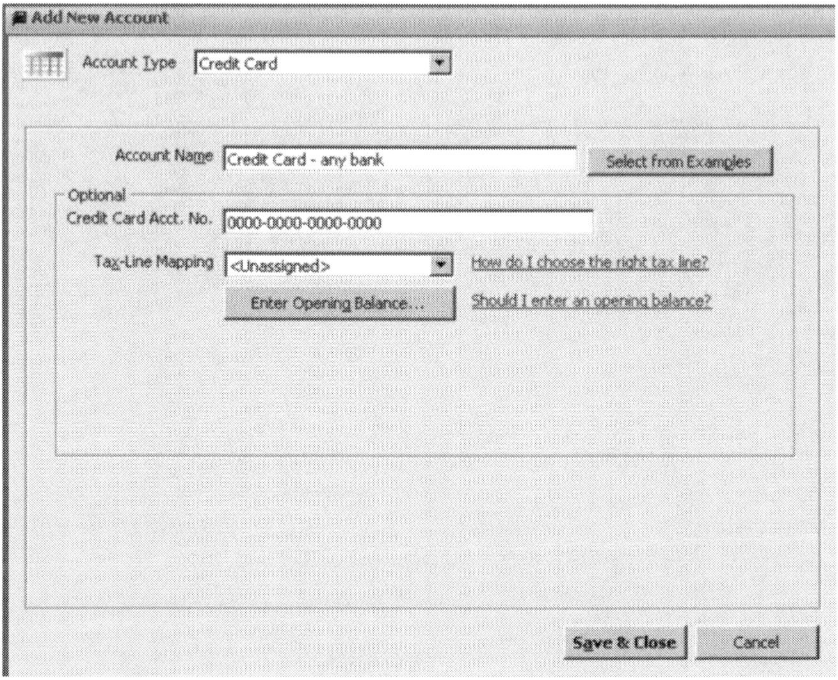

You will need to repeat the new account setup process for any loans you may have using the same opening balance criteria as the bank and credit card account setup.

When are you are done editing and or creating a new account click on "Save & Close."

Section Six: Setting Up Client Accounts

Now that the Chart of Accounts and all of the bank/ credit card/ loan accounts are set up, it is time to create your client accounts. Click on Customers--New in the left-hand column, or put your mouse over the Customers icon and click on "New."

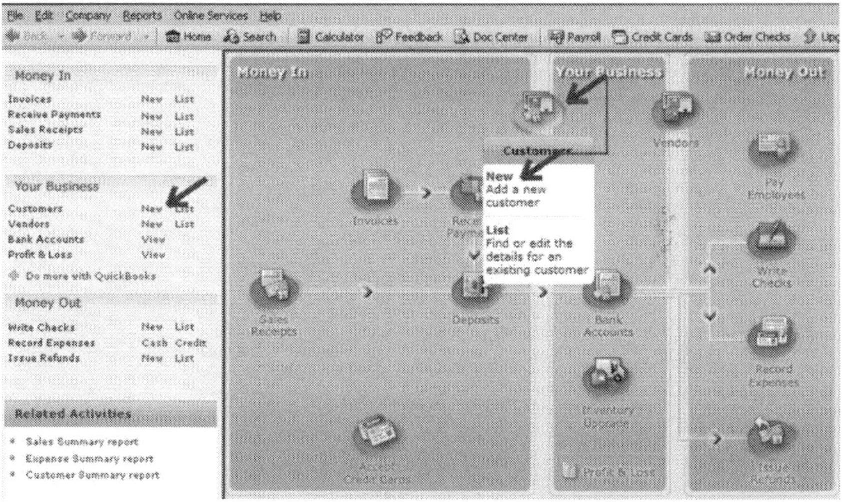

Fill in the information on the main screen, then click on the "Additional Info" tab and enter the payment terms. When you're done entering information, click on "OK." Client accounts can also be set up "on-the-fly" when entering client invoices.

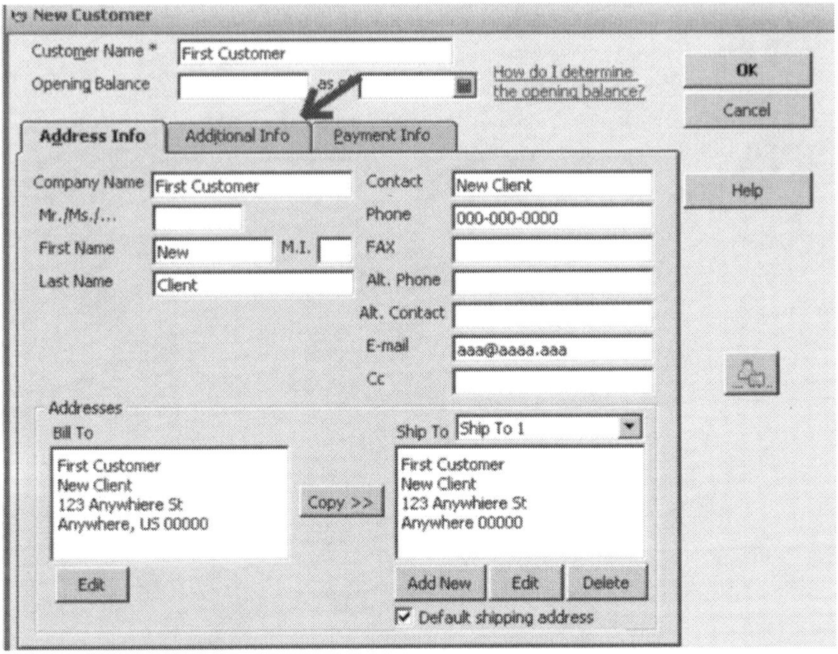

Section Seven: Setting Up Vendor Accounts

Creating your vendor accounts is a similar process to creating your client accounts. Click on Vendors--New in the left-hand column, or put your mouse over the "Vendors" icon and click on "New."

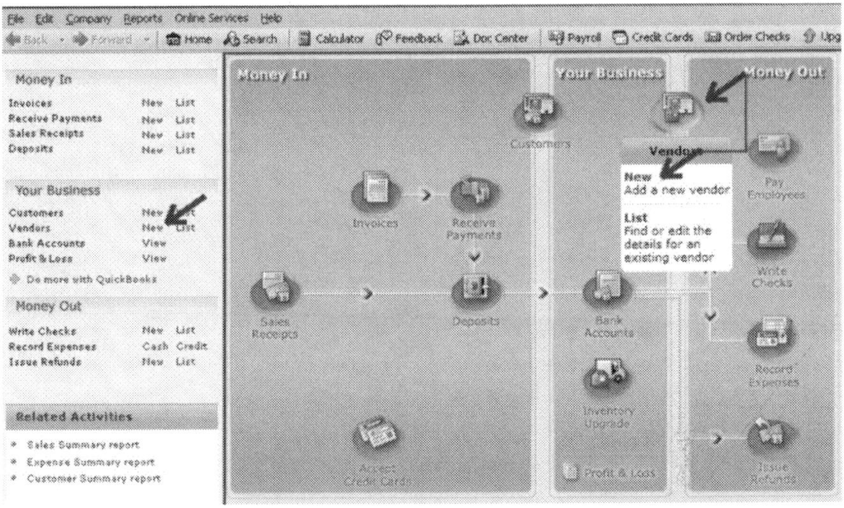

Fill in the information, and click "OK." Vendor accounts can also be set up "on-the-fly" when entering vendor invoices.

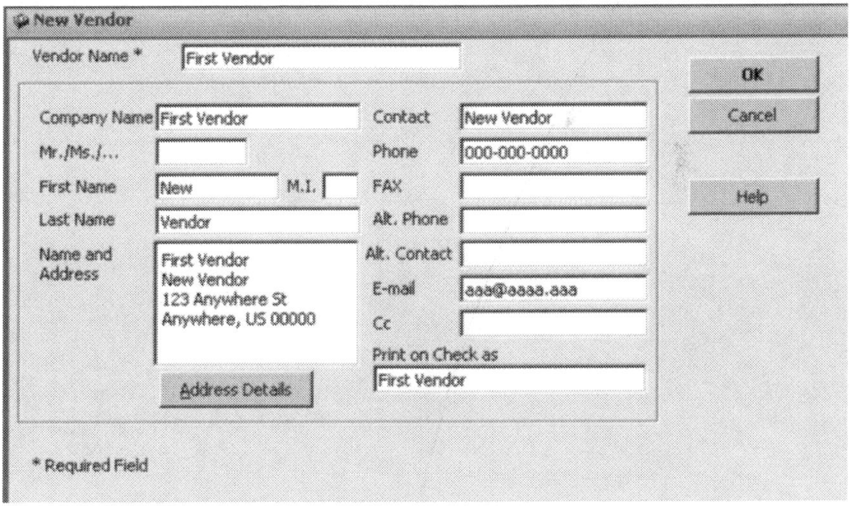

Obtaining Vendor Tax ID Information

If you have or are likely to pay more to a vendor than $600 during the fiscal year, you will need their Federal Tax ID Number (TIN) in order to issue them a 1099 at the end of the year (See Chapter 5--Section One). Either email or mail the vendor a W-9 Form (See Chapter 1--Section Four). Fill in the section marked with the darker (blue) arrow prior to sending it to the vendor; the vendor will complete the section marked with lighter (red) arrows, and send it back to you for your records. Once you receive the 1099 Form back from the vendor, file their completed W-9 with their Tax ID number in the Vendor's file.

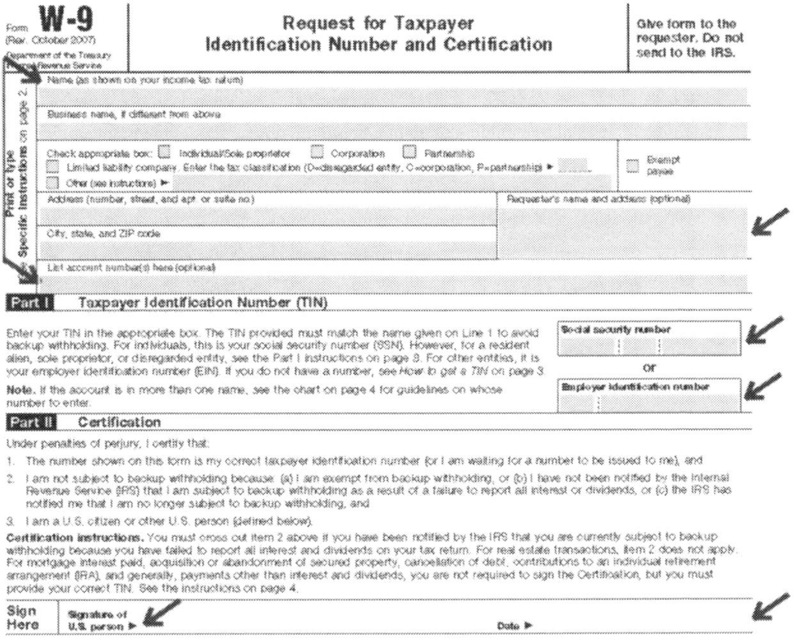
Form **W-9**
(Rev. October 2007)
Department of the Treasury
Internal Revenue Service

Request for Taxpayer Identification Number and Certification

Give form to the requester. Do not send to the IRS.

Print or type
Specific Instructions on page 2.

Name (as shown on your income tax return)

Business name, if different from above

Check appropriate box: ☐ Individual/Sole proprietor ☐ Corporation ☐ Partnership
☐ Limited liability company. Enter the tax classification (D=disregarded entity, C=corporation, P=partnership) ▶
☐ Other (see instructions) ▶
☐ Exempt payee

Address (number, street, and apt. or suite no.)

Requester's name and address (optional)

City, state, and ZIP code

List account number(s) here (optional)

Part I **Taxpayer Identification Number (TIN)**

Enter your TIN in the appropriate box. The TIN provided must match the name given on Line 1 to avoid backup withholding. For individuals, this is your social security number (SSN). However, for a resident alien, sole proprietor, or disregarded entity, see the Part I instructions on page 3. For other entities, it is your employer identification number (EIN). If you do not have a number, see *How to get a TIN* on page 3.

Note. If the account is in more than one name, see the chart on page 4 for guidelines on whose number to enter.

Social security number

or

Employer identification number

Part II **Certification**

Under penalties of perjury, I certify that:

1. The number shown on this form is my correct taxpayer identification number (or I am waiting for a number to be issued to me), and
2. I am not subject to backup withholding because: (a) I am exempt from backup withholding, or (b) I have not been notified by the Internal Revenue Service (IRS) that I am subject to backup withholding as a result of a failure to report all interest or dividends, or (c) the IRS has notified me that I am no longer subject to backup withholding, and
3. I am a U.S. citizen or other U.S. person (defined below).

Certification instructions. You must cross out item 2 above if you have been notified by the IRS that you are currently subject to backup withholding because you have failed to report all interest and dividends on your tax return. For real estate transactions, item 2 does not apply. For mortgage interest paid, acquisition or abandonment of secured property, cancellation of debt, contributions to an individual retirement arrangement (IRA), and generally, payments other than interest and dividends, you are not required to sign the Certification, but you must provide your correct TIN. See the instructions on page 4.

Sign Here | **Signature of U.S. person ▶** | **Date ▶**

Section Eight: Setting Up Billable Items

In order to invoice clients and to help track your income/expenses, QuickBooks Simple Start uses 'items' in the invoice system. We will go into creating invoices in Chapter 4, however, we will set up your tracking items now. Click on Company--Lists--Item List on the top menu.

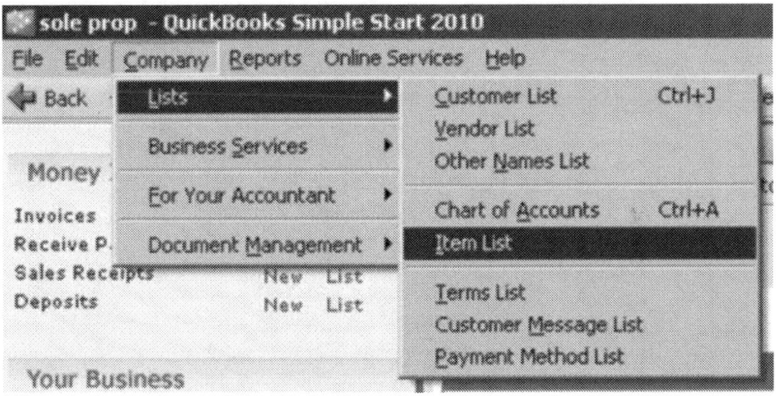

Right-click and select "New."

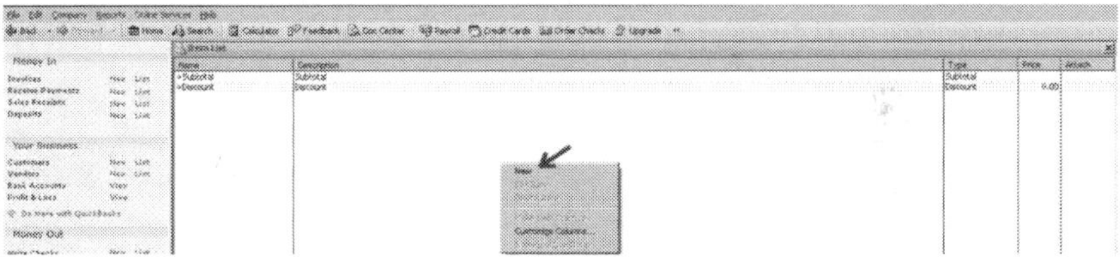

Now it is time to set up the items that you will invoice to your clients (e.g. services, photocopies, postage, etc.). Fill in the item name, a brief description, and a default price for that item.

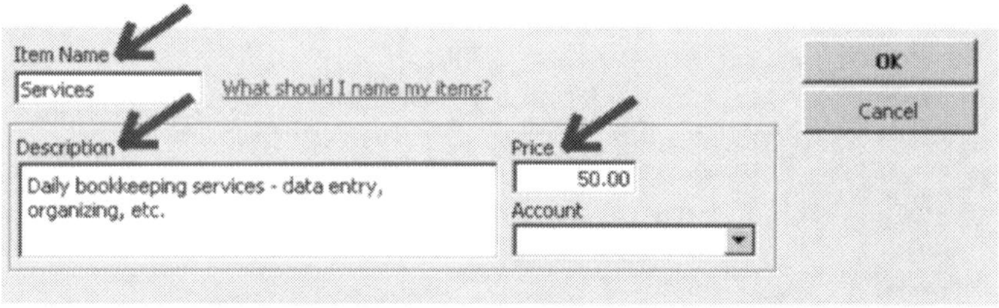

Next click on the drop-down box below "Account"; this will bring up a list from your Chart of Accounts. Select the appropriate account that matches the type of item you will be invoicing (e.g. the 'Postage' item would be associated with the 'postage' expense account).

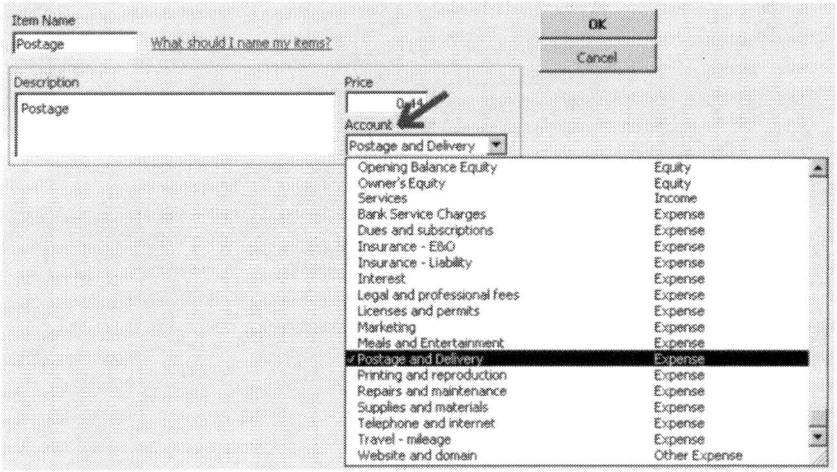

Note: If you will be accepting retainer payments or pre-payments from your clients, you will also need to set up a 'Retainer' item.

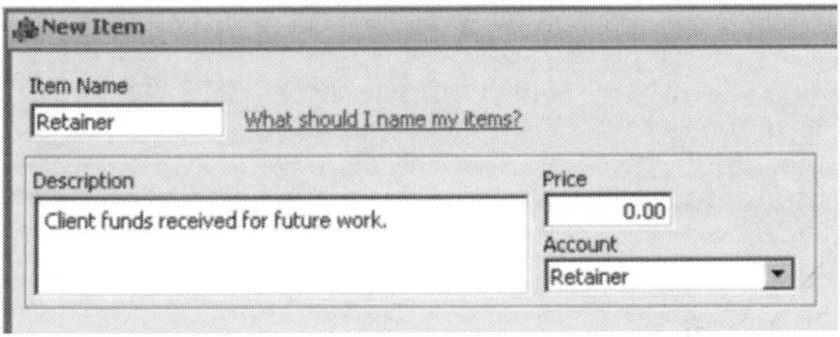

Click "OK" after setting up each item. Press ESC to return to the main menu when done.

Section Nine: Creating A General Journal Entry

General Journal entries are made to transfer balances between accounts (e.g., transferring money from checking to savings and vice versa.) Click on Company--For Your Accountant--Make General Journal Entries. You will need this information later when actually making the entries.

Section Ten: Setting Up A Petty Cash Fund *(optional)*

You may wish to have a 'Petty Cash' fund that you use for small expenses for which you don't wish to write a check or use a credit card (e.g. tolls, parking meters, etc.). This account will normally have less than $100 in it and will be reconciled monthly. To add funds to petty cash, you will need to either cash a check for the opening balance of your petty fund account or use personal funds to create your petty cash account rather than cashing a check from your business account. If you cash a business check Quickbooks Simple Start will enter the debits/credits for you. If you use personal funds to setup petty cash, you will make a general journal entry to record the transaction.

Click on Company--For Your Accountant--Make General Journal Entries. Enter the accounts as you see below (substituting the amount for the actual amount you are putting in the petty cash fund). A debit to "Cash on Hand" will increase the petty cash fund and a credit to "Owner's Equity" will make the balancing entry to that account.

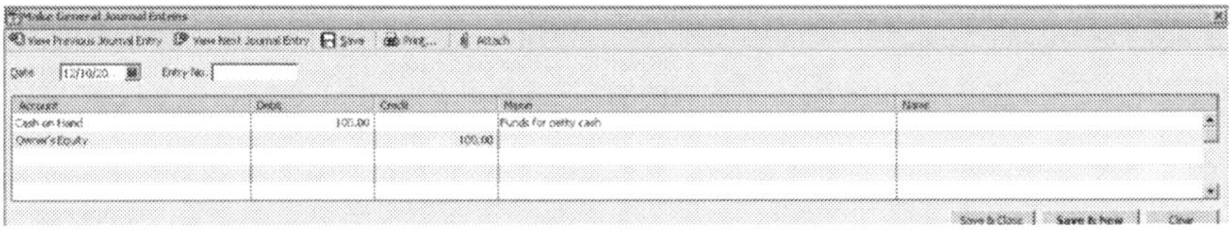

You will need to create a General Journal entry any time you add personal funds to your petty cash fund.

Keep your petty cash funds separate from your personal money. I recommend using either an envelope or a small cash box for the petty cash funds/receipts.

Section Eleven: Tax Records

Federal Estimated Tax Deposits are due April 15, July 15, September 15, and January 15. The income tax deposit should be ¼ of your estimated annual income tax liability based on your annual NET income (income less expenses) for the year. For beginning sole proprietors and LLCs, I recommend you deposit 18% of your estimated annual net income (this is the amount automatically calculated on the Annual Budget Worksheet) for Federal income taxes.

Self Employment (Social Security/Medicare) Tax Deposits should be made at the same time as the Federal Income Tax deposits. The self employment tax deposit should be ¼ of your estimated annual self employment tax liability based on your annual NET income (income less expenses) for the year.

To calculate your self-employment deposit, start by multiplying your estimated annual net income by 0.9235 (92.35%). (If this amount is less than $400, you don't have to pay self-employment tax.) Now multiply the amount of your net earnings up to $76,200 by 0.153 (15.3%), and multiply any net earnings over $76,200 by 0.029 (2.9%). Add your two numbers together. This is your estimated annual self-employment tax. (This amount is also automatically calculated on the Annual Budget Worksheet.)

Deposits are made to the IRS through E.F.T.P.S. (https://www.eftps.com/eftps/) which will need to be set up at least two weeks prior to when your first deposit is due. You will set up your E.F.T.P.S. account online using <u>your name</u> and social security number if you are a sole proprietor, LLC, or partnership; you will use your <u>*company*</u> <u>name</u> and EIN number if you are incorporated.

Check with your State for their estimated tax deposit requirements (if any) and the process of making those deposits. I recommend you put aside 7% of your estimated annual net income (this is the amount automatically calculated on the Annual Budget Worksheet) for State taxes.

In addition, you will need to send 1099s to any non-incorporated vendor to whom you pay more than $600 annually; a copy of the 1099 also goes to the IRS. (See Chapter 5--Section One.) The deadlines for 1099s are:

January 31 – 1099-MISC to subcontractors/vendors
February 28 – Federal 1096/1099-MISC to the IRS.

Section Twelve: Setting Up An Electronic Filing System

Client Records and Vendor Records should be scanned and kept in an electronic format as well as a paper filing system. In addition, keep all e-mails and IMs from your clients in an electronic format as well as printing them out for a hard copy backup.

Use a standard filing tree to maintain your files:

Clients

[Client Name] (each client should have their own file)

Accounting files

Bills

Deposits

Receipts

Correspondence

Invoices/Statements

Vendors

[Vendor Name] (each vendor should have their own file)

Bills

Correspondence

Section Thirteen: Setting Up a Paper Filing System

Your paper system will look very similar to your electronic system. Use manila file folders to create client files, vendor files, bank and credit card files, etc. Paper files should be organized in the following order:

- Current receivables (unpaid client invoices)
  - Once the client pays their bill, mark the invoice "paid" and move it to the client's file.
- Current payables (bills you owe)
  - Once you pay the bill, mark the invoice "Paid" and move it to the vendor's file. Mark the invoice with "Amount, Check #, and Date" on it. (I had a custom rubber stamp made.)
- Credit card receipts (current month)
  - After reconciling your credit card at the end of the month, put the receipts in an envelope and attach it to the credit card statement (See Chapter 4--Section Six) and move the statement/envelope to the credit card account file.
- Current Cash receipts (cash paid out for the current month instead of writing a check or using a credit card, i.e. petty cash/cash on hand)
  - After reconciling petty cash at the end of the month, attach the receipts to the "petty cash form" (See

Chapter 4--Section Six) and move the form/receipts to the Petty Cash file.

- Tax deposit record copies
  - Use a divider in the file to separate Federal and State tax deposit records
- Client files for each client (contract, notes, e-mails, IMs, paid invoices, etc.)
- Timesheets for previous months
- Bank checking statements (reconciled)
- Savings account statements (reconciled)
- Credit card statements (reconciled)
- Vendor files for each vendor (invoices you have paid, correspondence, etc.)
- Petty cash/cash on hand receipts (reconciled)
- 1099/1096 forms issued to vendors
- 1099 forms received from client

Chapter 4

Creating and Maintaining Bookkeeping Records

Section One: Accounts Receivable (Clients)

Creating Client Invoices

Once you have completed work for a client, you need to create an invoice in order to request payment. Click on Invoices--New in the left-hand column, or put your mouse over the Invoices icon and click on "New." Either process will bring up a new invoice form.

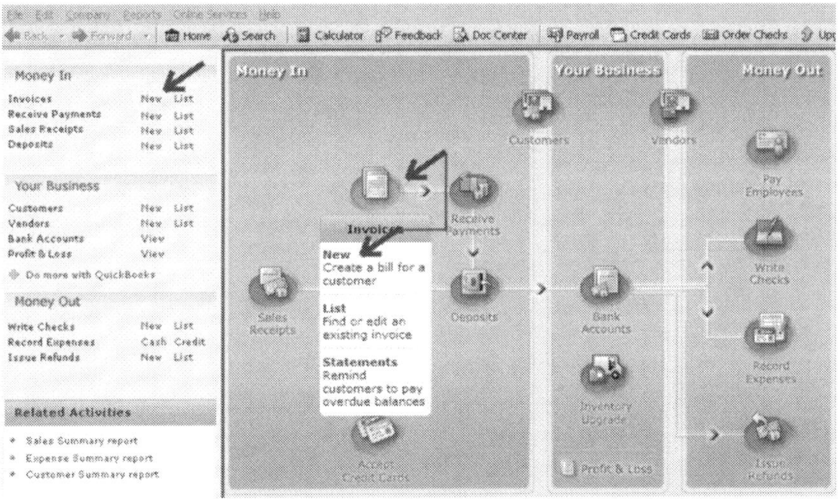

Clicking the "Customer" drop-down box and either select an existing client or click on 'Add New' to create one (See Chapter 3--Section Six).

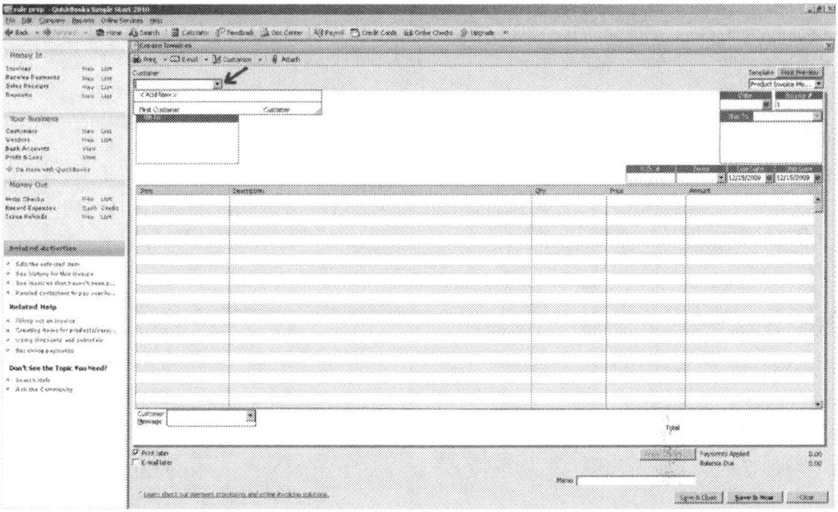

When you select a current customer from the drop-down box, the customer's contact and terms information will automatically fill in on the invoice.

The invoice date will default to today's date and the due date will be calculated based on the payment terms. You can enter payment terms now if you did not set them up as part of the client file, or if they have changed. The invoice number will start at 1; you can manually change this, as well.

Next, you will select an item to bill from the dropdown box. If the item you wish to bill is not in the list, click on 'Add New' and create the item (See Chapter 3--Section Eight). Fill in the quantity (Qty). The price will default to the item's setting; you can manually override the price if necessary. The amount will automatically calculate for you. Repeat until all billable items are listed on the invoice.

Below is an example of a completed Invoice Form – ready to print/pdf and send to your client.

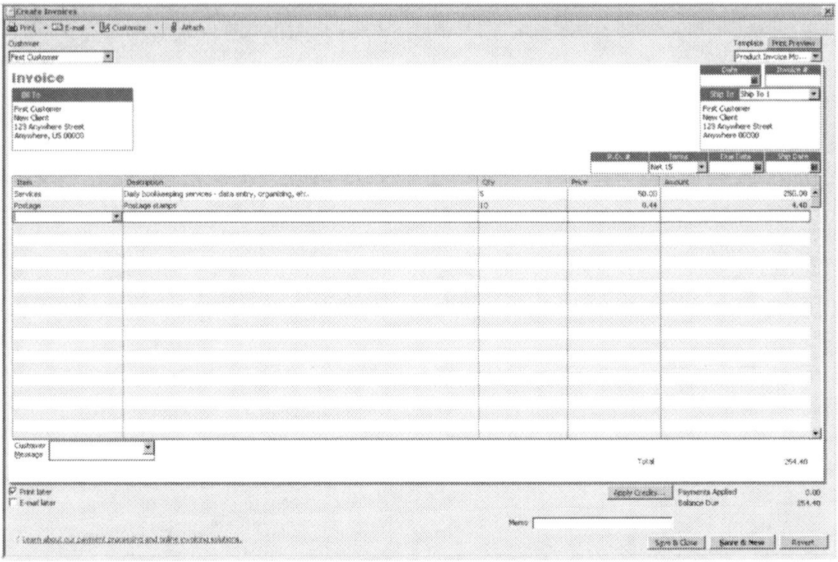

Click on Print or Email to process the invoice for your client. 'Print' your invoices to a pdf file which can then be saved to, and emailed to the client from, the client's electronic file (See Chapter 3--Section Twelve). You will be prompted to save any changes to the client file prior to printing or saving the invoice.

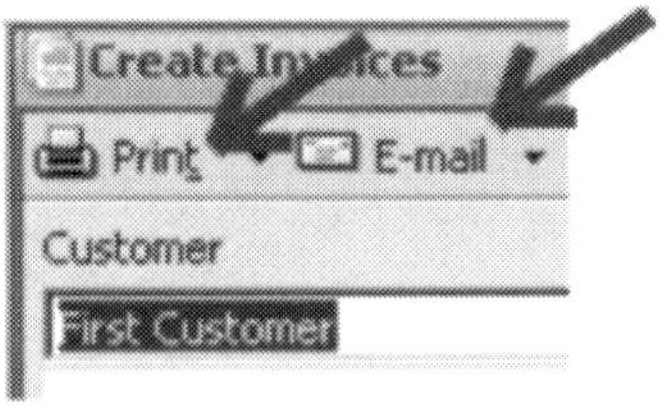

Click 'Save & Close' when you are done creating and printing the invoice.

Tracking Client Payments Due

Now that you have invoiced your clients, you will wish to keep track of when their payment(s) are due to you. QuickBooks Simple Start has a few easy ways of doing this. You can run the "Invoices That Haven't Been Paid" report:

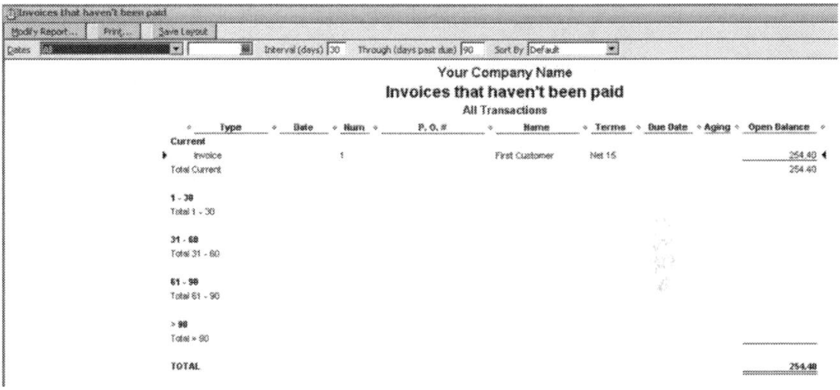

Or, alternatively you can use the "Invoices--List" report. Click on Invoice--List in the left-hand column, or put your mouse over the Invoice icon and click on "List."

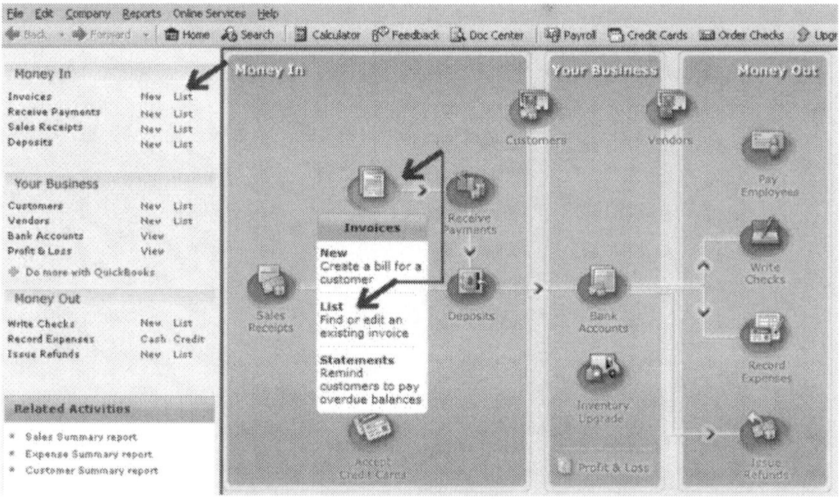

This will open a window with a list of <u>all</u> invoices in the system. Click on the drop down list next to "Filter By" and select "Open Invoices." You will now have only a list of customers that currently owe you money. The Due Date and Aging fields will tell you when the invoice is/was due, and there is a running total at the bottom of the list for all outstanding invoices.

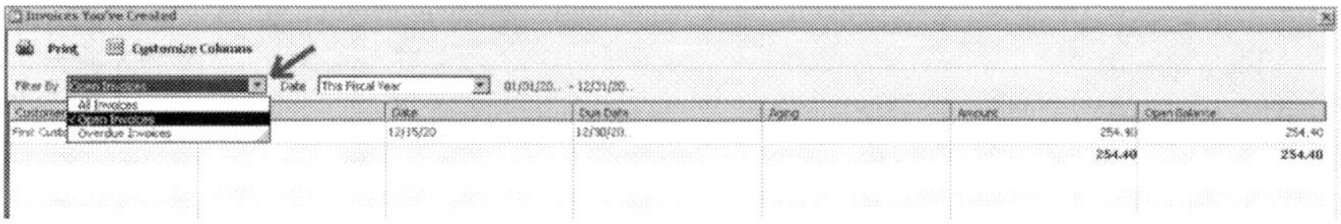

Issuing a Statement to the Client

On occasion, you may have a client invoice that becomes past due. In that circumstance, you will want to issue a past-due statement reminder to the client. Prior to issuing the statement, you will need to create an invoice for past-due charges/late fees (if they are built into your contract, of course!). Once the past-due charges invoice is in place, put your mouse over the Invoice icon and click on "Statements."

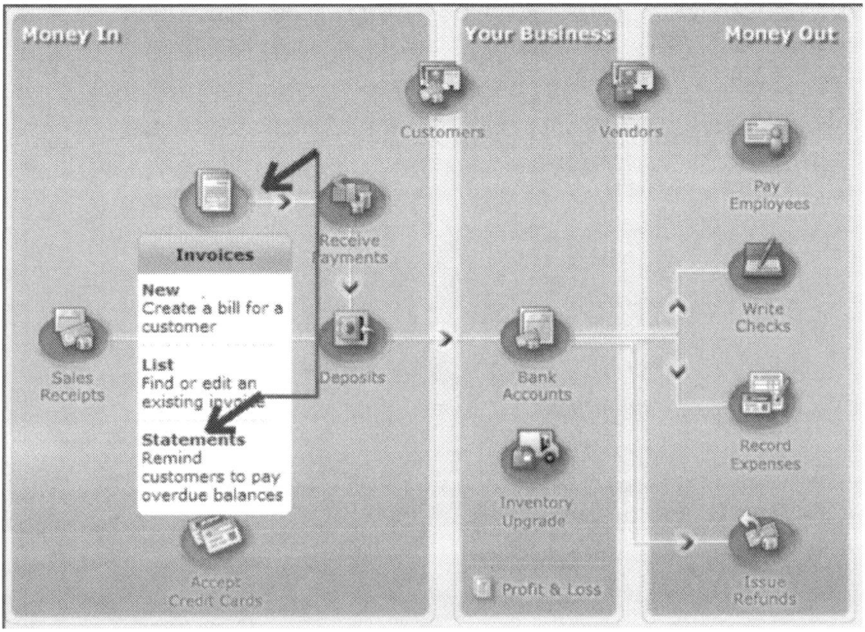

The statement date field defaults to the current date and the statement period defaults to the past thirty day period; these dates can be manually changed. Click on "Do not create statements with a zero balance" or you will get ALL statements in the date range, including current and paid ones. Select "one customer" and the current client list will open; choose the past due client for whom you wish to issue a statement.

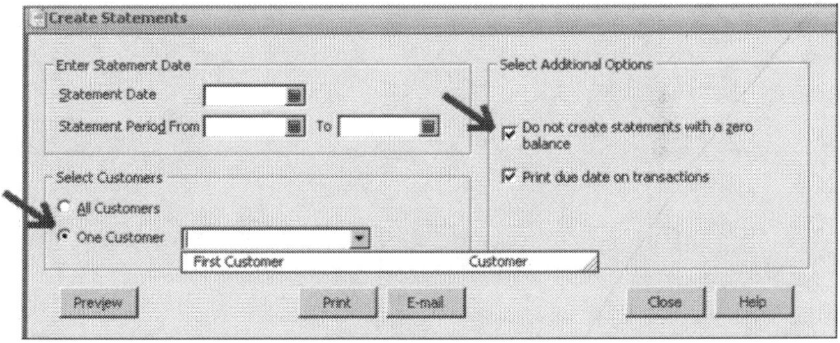

Click on "Preview" to see the client statement. Clicking on "Print" will send the statement to your default printer; you may wish to set your default printer to print to pdf before issuing statements (be sure and save a copy of the client statement in your electronic client file).

Recording Client Payments

When you receive a payment from your client you will need to record it to clear the invoice. Click on Receive Payments--New in the left-hand column, or put your mouse over the "Receive Payments" icon and click on "New."

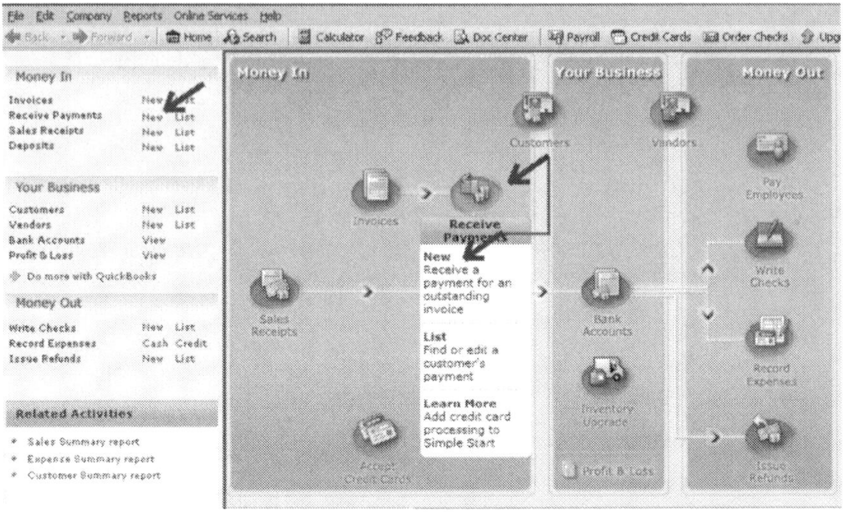

Click on the "Received From" dropdown list and locate the name of the client who made the payment.

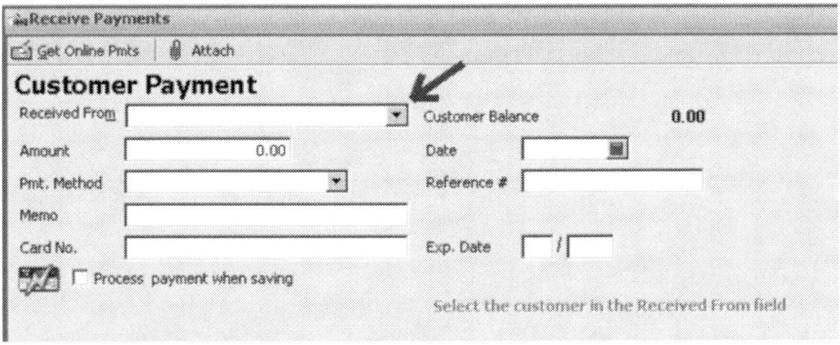

The client balance and list of their open invoices will now be on the screen. Fill in the amount received (A) and choose a payment method from the dropdown list (B). Now click on the invoice that is being paid (C); note that a checkmark will automatically appear next to the first invoice. If the payment was less than the invoice amount, decide if the amount is an underpayment or should be written off (D).

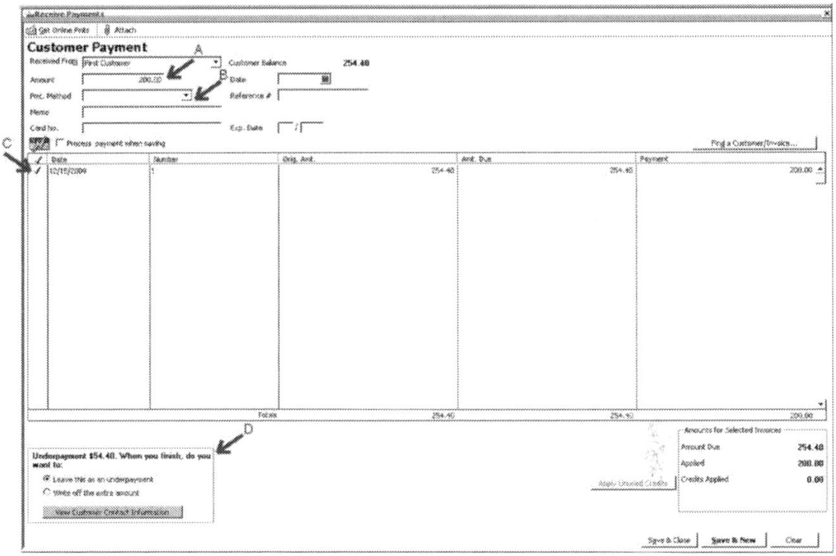

Click on "Save & Close" when you are done with the entry.

Recording Bank Deposits

After receiving funds from a client, you will deposit them to your bank account by making a deposit, transferring them from PayPal, etc. To record these deposits to the QuickBooks Simple Start bank account register click on Deposits--New in the left-hand column, or put your mouse over the "Deposits" icon and click on "New."

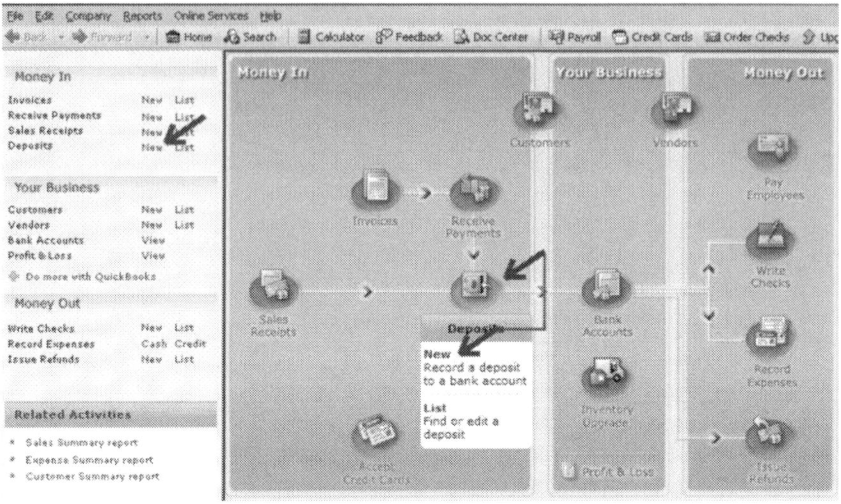

Verify the account to which the deposit was made (checking, savings, etc.) then click on the payment(s) that were deposited. Click on "OK."

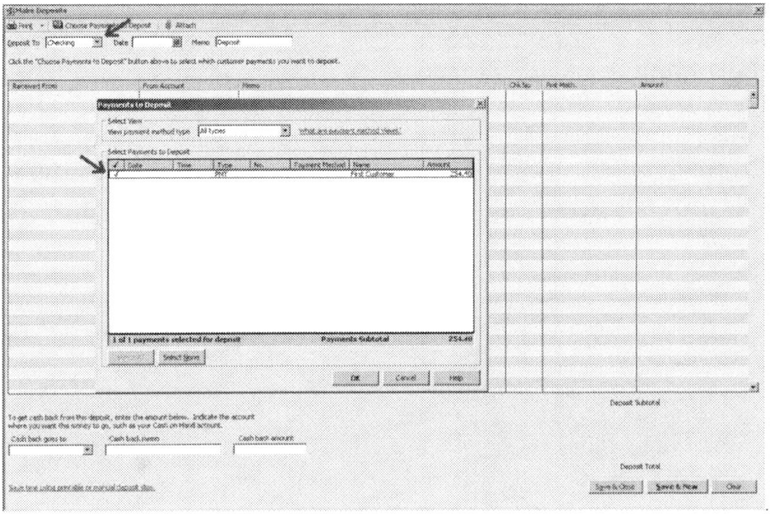

Verify the amount of the deposit being recorded and click on "Save & Close" when you are done.

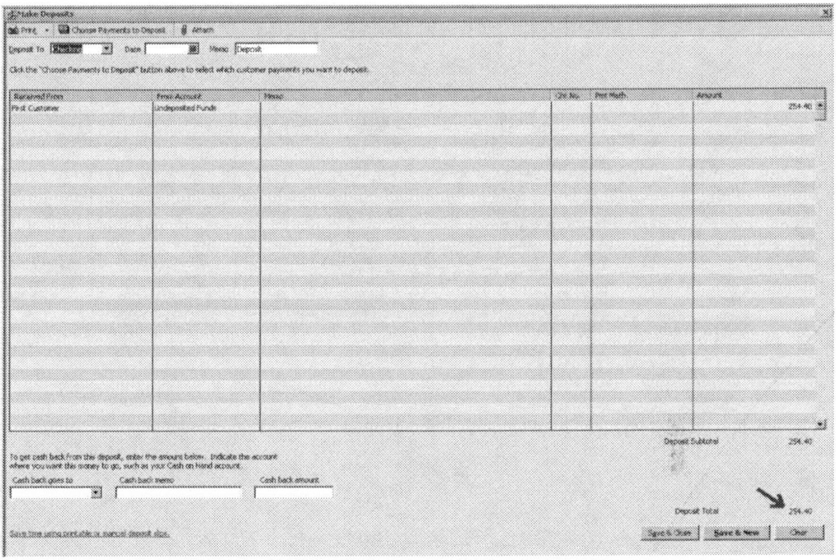

Because each deposit will show up as a single amount on the bank statement rather than individual payments, record individual checks from each deposit on a "Deposit Reconciliation Form" to make bank reconciliation easier at the end of the month. The total deposit is the amount that will be listed on the bank account reconciliation page. Photocopy your client's checks and attach the copies to your deposit reconciliation form, as well.

EXAMPLE OF DEPOSIT RECONCILIATION FORM (Excel

Invoice Payments

Date Deposited

1/1/20..

Client Name	$ Deposited
Character	275.00
PIC	135.00
Total Deposit	$410.00

Reconcile

Cash	0.00
Checks	410.00
Total	410.00
Diff.	$0.00

Retainer Clients - Recording Retainer Funds

The process is slightly different for retainer clients. You will start by creating a 'Sales Receipt' to record the client's deposit to their account.

Click on Sales Receipt--New in the left-hand column, or put your mouse over the "Sales Receipt" icon and click on "New."

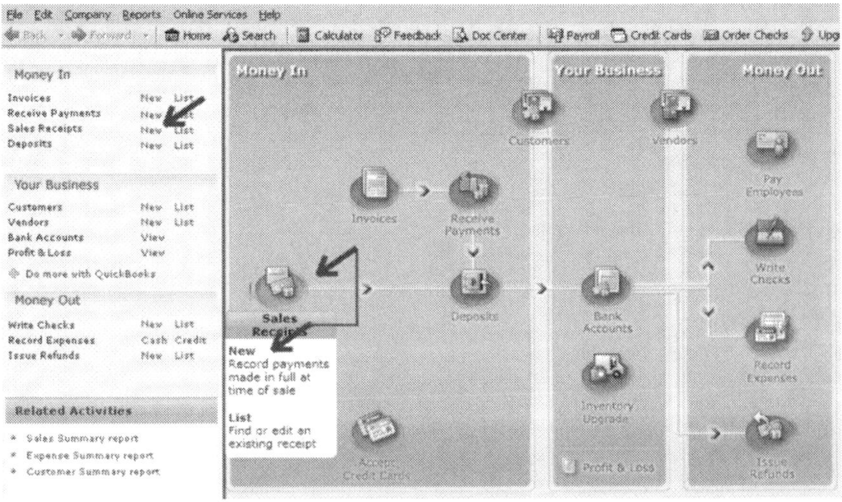

The first time you set up a sales receipt you will see this box:

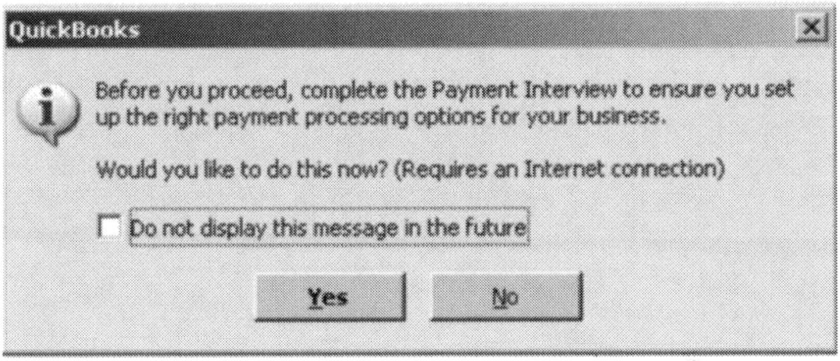

ONLY Click on 'Yes' and follow the prompts if you wish to accept credit cards or over-the-phone checks through QuickBooks. Otherwise, click in the "Do not display this message in the future" box and then click on 'No.'

Sales receipts are set up almost identically to an invoice. The primary difference being that your only item will be "Retainer." It is not necessary to enter the quantity, only the amount of money received from the client; the quantity will default to 1. Print/pdf the sales receipt and put it in your electronic client file (in the client's 'invoice' folder). Click "Save & Close" when you are done.

Here is a completed "sales receipt" for recording a client deposit:

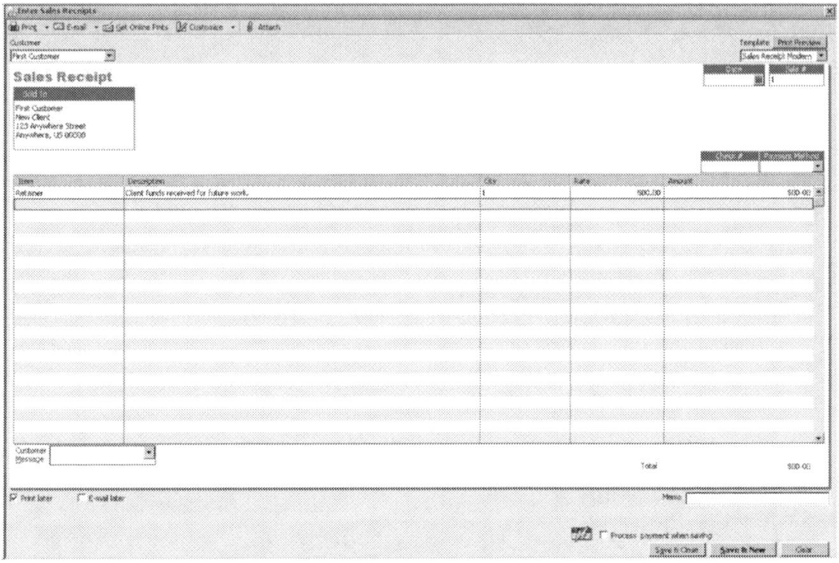

Next, you will deposit the funds into your bank account and record the deposit in the same way you would a paid invoice. (See Chapter 4--*Section One.)*

Tracking Retainer Funds

You will want to keep track of how much money you have for each client that has pre-paid your service fees and/or expenses so that you don't deduct more from the retainer account than has been paid and, if necessary, so you know to request additional funds from the client. Click on CTRL-A or go to Company--lists--chart of accounts. Once your chart of accounts opens up, double click on "Retainer" to open the account.

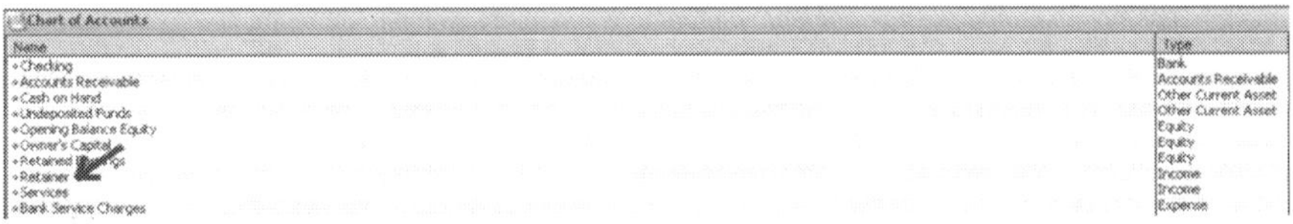

There is no easy way in QuickBooks Simple Start to see totals by company. You will need to manually add up each client's deposits and subtract their withdrawals to get an accurate balance by client.

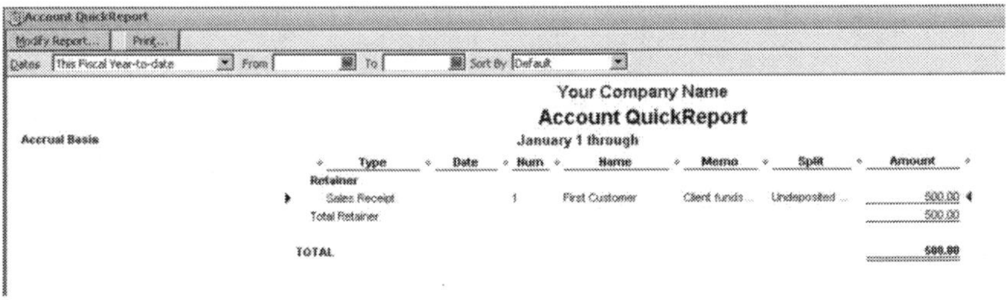

Press the ESC key to return to the main menu.

Clearing Retainer Funds

Once you have completed work for the client, you will need to clear the retainer account. To do this, *create an invoice as if you were billing the client*. After entering all billable items, add the "Retainer" item with a *negative* amount equal to the total on the invoice.

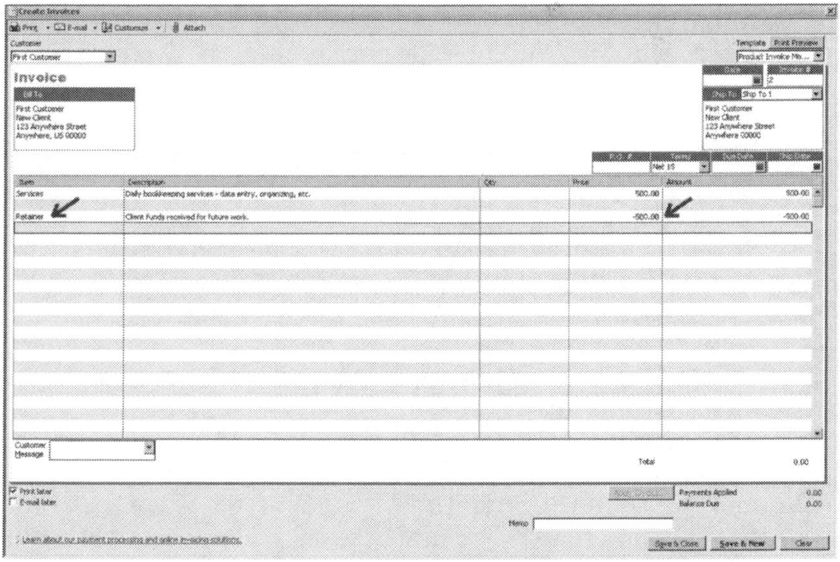

The invoice will now show as 'paid' and the funds will be removed from the client's retainer account balance.

When you look at the Retainer account (CTRL-A, double-click "Retainer") you will see the adjustment to reduce the funds in the account.

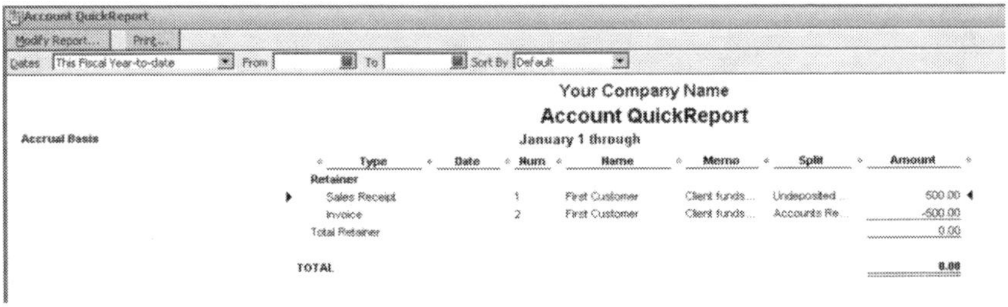

Press the ESC key to return to the main menu.

Section Two: Accounts Payable (Vendors

Tracking Receipts For Purchases

Keep all receipts for any purchase you make, whether a physical or online purchase. If there is no receipt available, (e.g. parking meters) create a hand-written 'receipt' with the date, amount, and vendor name on it. Write on the back of each receipt what the receipt is for (supplies, marketing, etc.) and for what job the items were purchased (if applicable). You will need these if your tax return is audited by the IRS.

Keep your current credit card receipts in a separate folder so that they are easy to find when you reconcile your credit card statement.

Keep regular vendor receipts in the vendor's physical file as well as scanning them for the vendor's electronic file. Create a separate file for one-time vendors, both physically and electronically. The scanned receipt file is named by Vendor Name in the One-Time Vendors file. If you get more than 3 receipts for any vendor, create a vendor-specific file for them.

Entering Bills To Be Paid

Click on Write Checks--New in the left-hand column, or put your mouse over the "Write Checks" icon and click on "New."

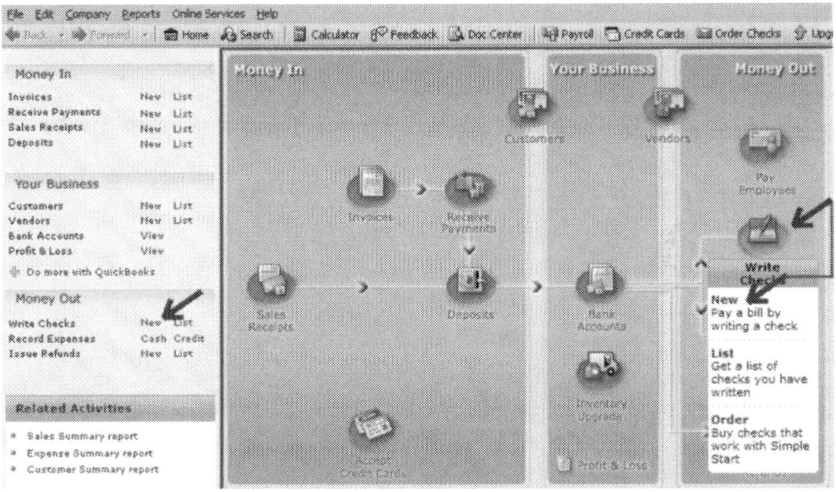

You can either type in the Vendor Name or click on the dropdown box to select a vendor (A). If the vendor doesn't exist, either type in the name of the vendor and choose "Set Up" then choose "Vendor" or click on "Add New" in the vendor dropdown box to create a new vendor (See Chapter 3--Section Seven).

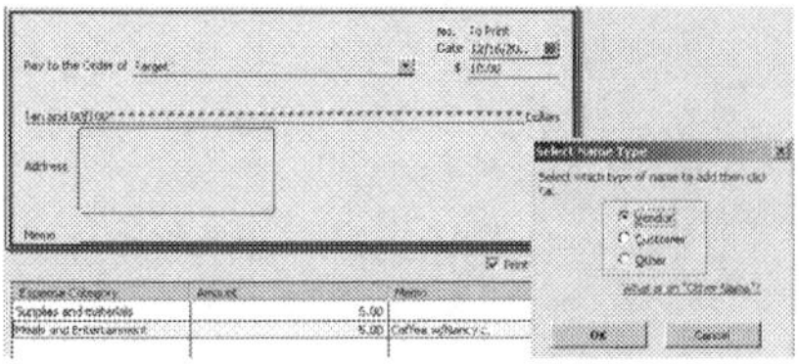

Next enter the amount of the bill (B). The invoice number goes on the "Memo" line (C). Click on the "Expense Category" dropdown box (D) and choose the correct expense category. Repeat 'D' for multiple categories on the same vendor invoice. Enter the amount of each item in the "Amount" column next to the corresponding expense.

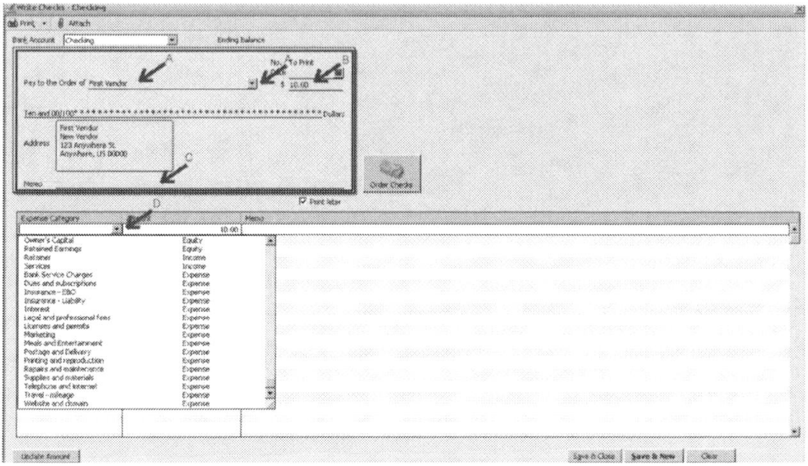

Click on "Save & Close" when you are done.

IMPORTANT TO NOTE: When you enter a check even marked "Print later" the amount will be automatically deducted from your QuickBooks Simple Start bank check register.

Tracking bills to be paid

There are several different ways to track what bills have been entered and not yet paid. Click on Write Checks--List in the left-hand menu, or put your mouse over the "Write Checks" icon and click on "List." Items without check numbers *should be* unpaid bills.

Click on File--Print Forms--Checks and see what checks show up in the "Select Checks to Print" box (be sure and close without printing).

Or, the easiest way, is through your QuickBooks Simple Start checking account register. To open your checking account register, click on Bank Accounts--View in the left-hand menu, or put your mouse over the Bank Accounts icon, click on "View" (A), and choose your checking account from the dropdown list (B).

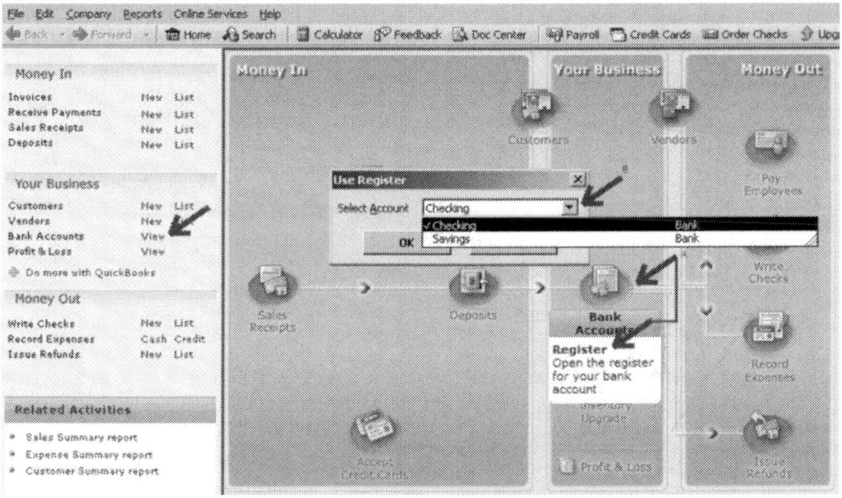

Once the check register is open, look for 'To Print' in the "Number Type" column (A). Again, note that even though the check number is 'To Print', the amount was deducted from your QuickBooks Simple Start checking account register. The items marked "To Print" will always be the last entries in your check register. To see the current balance, look at the balance *prior to* the "To Print" entries (B). Press the ESC key to return to the main menu.

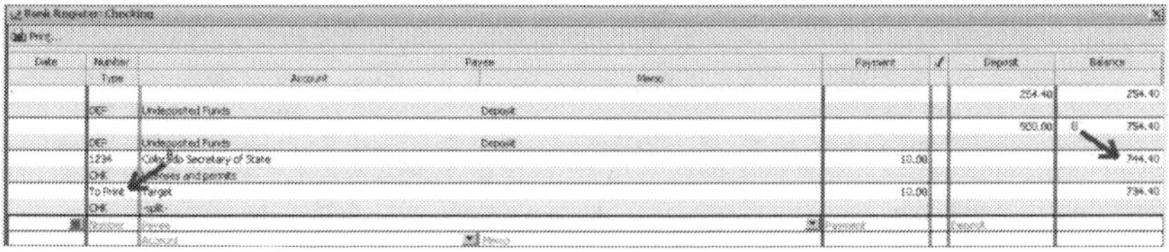

Paying your bills

Printing Checks With QuickBooks Simple Start

If you choose to print your checks through QuickBooks Simple Start, you will need to purchase printer-compatible checks. You can obtain these through Intuit (makers of QuickBooks) by clicking on "Order Checks" in the "Write Checks" screen, or through a traditional check printing service (use Google to find them). To print checks from QuickBooks Simple Start, click on File--Print Forms--Checks. (This page will also show you what bills are pending payment). The following screens will walk you through the process.

Verify the bank account, enter the first check number to be printed, and click on each check you wish to print (or click "Select All"). Click on "OK."

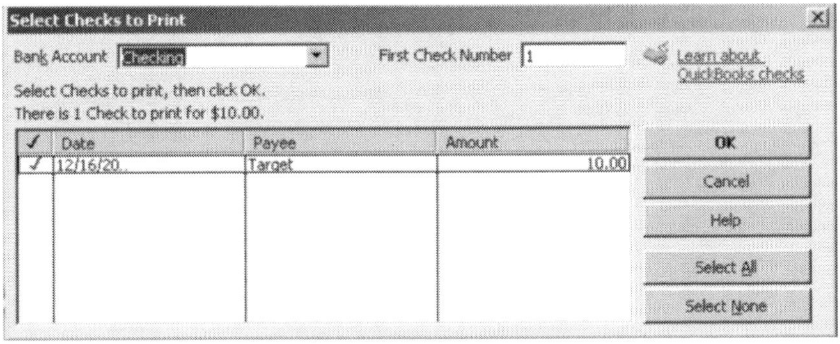

Use the dropdown menu to choose your printer. Check style will be determined by what type of printer-ready checks you purchased. Click on "Print." If your checks print properly, click on "OK" on the "Print Checks - Confirmation" page. Done!

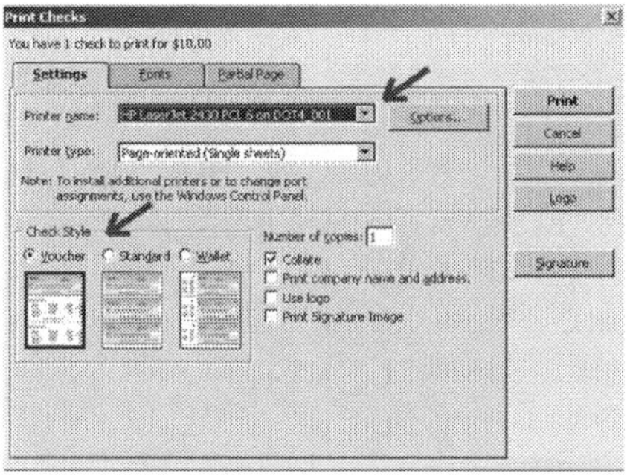

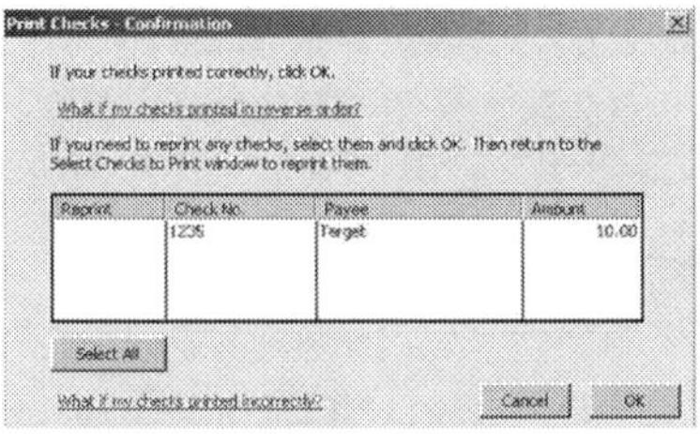

Recording a Hand-written Check or EFT Payment

Follow the same process as *Entering Bills to be Paid*. Unclick "Print Later" (A) and enter the check number that was written (B); for Electronic (online) payments use "EFT" for the check number.

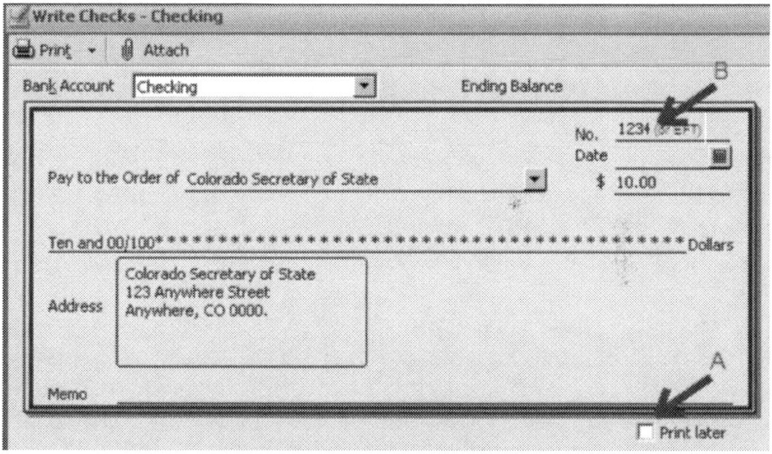

Clearing Bills Entered In the Check Register But Paid by A Hand-written Check

Open your check register (See Chapter 4--Section Two). Double click "To Print" in the "Number Type" column of the item you paid. Replace "To Print" with the correct check number, verify the date the check was written and change it if necessary. Click "Record." Press the ESC key to return to the main menu.

Section Three: Transferring Funds from Checking To Savings

If you look at the "Annual Budget and Bill Tracking Worksheet" (See Chapter 3--Section Two), you will see that funds should be transferred from checking to savings each month for items such as supplies, marketing, equipment and software purchases, and estimated tax deposits. To do this, you will create a General Journal entry that records this transfer. (See Chapter 3--Section Nine)

Click on Company--For Your Accountant--Make General Journal Entries. Enter the accounts as you see below. A debit to "Savings" will increase the savings account and a credit to "Checking" will decrease the checking account.

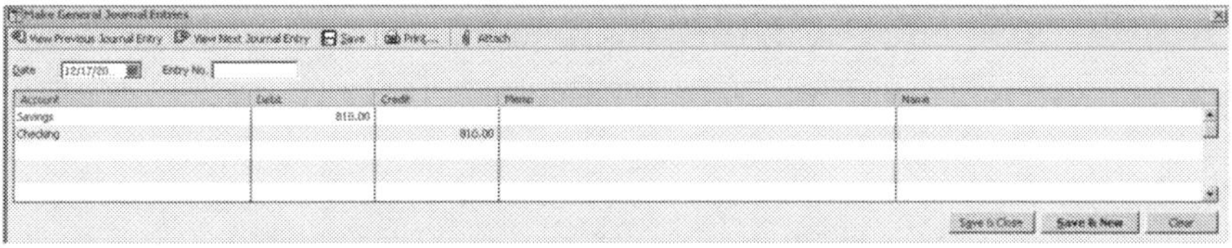

When you transfer funds back from savings to checking to pay for supplies, taxes, etc., the entries will need to be made in reverse order (i.e. Checking will be debited and the expense account will be credited).

QuickBooks Simple Start does not have a system for creating sub-accounts to track the purpose the money was transferred between savings and checking accounts. Therefore, you will need a separate tracking sheet to record the amount of funds for the various accounts.

Enter the date, the amount being transferred into/out of savings AND the account (the savings entry must match the total of the accounts entries on the same line. The total in the "Savings" column (A) should match the actual amount in your savings account. The "Diff between transfer and balances entered" (B) should always be zero; this is a cross-check to be sure that the savings amount and the categories amount always matches. Remember to log any expenses transferred back to checking as a negative amount (C).

EXAMPLE OF SAVINGS ACCOUNT LEDGER FORM (Excel

Savings Account Ledger

			BALANCES				
					SE Tax	SE Tax	Diff between transfer and
Date	Savings	Supplies	Marketing	Equip/Software	FEDERAL	STATE	balances entered
1/31	810.00	50.00	169.00	169.00	304.00	118.00	
2/10	-15.00	-15.00					
2/28	468.00		104.00	104.00	187.00	73.00	
3/31	725.00		161.00	161.00	290.00	113.00	
4/6	-75.00		-75.00				
4/15	-861.00	-20.00			-841.00		
4/30	820.00	50.00	171.00	171.00	308.00	120.00	
	1,872.00	65.00	530.00	605.00	248.00	424.00	

When you need to use some of the savings funds 'earmarked' for a specific purpose, transfer the necessary amount from savings back into checking, make a general journal entry in QuickBooks Simple Start, and make a matching entry into the Savings Account Ledger. The current savings account balance in the Savings Account Ledger should ALWAYS match the balance in the QuickBooks Simple Start Savings register AND in your actual bank savings account.

Section Four: Entering Petty Cash/Credit Card Transactions

Using a "Petty Cash Reconciliation Form" for the purpose of tracking and entering petty cash receipts into QuickBooks Simple Start makes tracking petty cash fairly easy. Place all current monthly receipts into a manila folder as you receive them (See Chapter 4--Section Two), and then at the end of the month input them into the reconciliation form and enter them into QuickBooks Simple Start.

EXAMPLE OF PETTY CASH RECONCILIATION FORM (Excel)

1-Jan				
EXPENSES				
Date	**Expense**	**G/L**	**Job**	**Amt**
12-Jan	Parking meter - downtown	Travel-Parking	Character	1.75
			Total Expenses	1.75

Cash on Hand	98.25
Total Expenses	1.75
Balance in QB	100.00
Difference	-

To make petty cash entries into QuickBooks Simple Start, click on Record Expenses--Cash in the left-hand column, or put your mouse over the "Record Expenses" icon and click on "Cash."

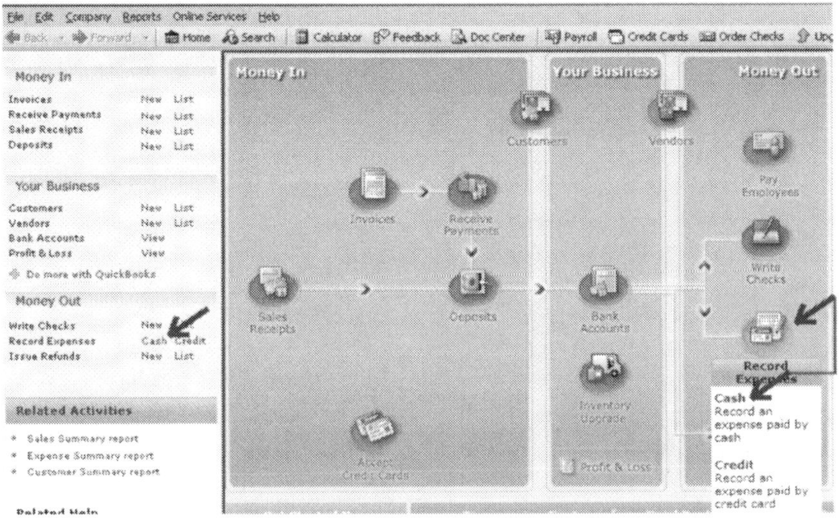

You will see the General Journal entry you made to put funds into the "petty cash (cash on hand)" fund (A). Under "Payee" enter the vendor's name or use the dropdown box to find the vendor's name where you spent the cash (B), click on the dropdown box under "Expense" to find the appropriate expense category (C), and enter the amount spent under "Decrease" (D). QuickBooks Simple Start will automatically create a new journal entry with this information in it. Click on "Record" when you are done making entries.

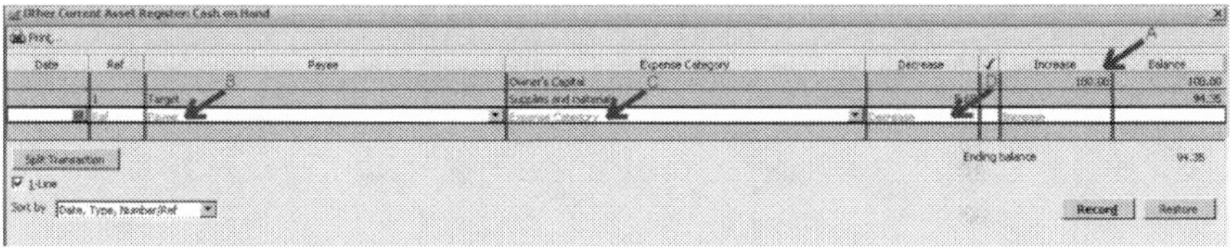

Follow these same instructions to enter credit card transactions using "Record Expenses--Credit" instead of "Record Expenses--Cash."

To create a credit card reconciliation form, download your credit card items from the online statement into Excel, and add columns to the right for 'G/L" (general journal) and "Job." Match your credit card receipts to the statement items, filling in the expense (G/L) category, and the job as you match the receipt to the charge. Subtotal by job and then G/L to make a quick entry form.

TRANS DA	POST DA	DESCRIPTION	AMT	G/L	JOB
7/31/20..	8/3/20..	USPS	5.50	Postage	PIC
8/3/20..	8/4/20..	CO SECTY OF STATE	10.00	Licenses	TVOG
8/10/20..	8/11/20..	OFFICEMAX	24.27	Ofc Spply	TVOG
8/11/20..	8/12/20..	USPS	8.80	Postage	PIC
			48.57		
			14.30	Postage	PIC
			10.00	Licenses	TVOG
			24.27	Ofc Spply	TVOG
			48.57		

Section Five: Calculating and Making Tax Deposits

Federal Tax Deposits

Quarterly Net Federal Tax Deposits: Estimated Tax Deposits (both Income and Self Employment) are due April 15, July 15, September 15, and January 15. Each deposit should be ¼ of your estimated annual tax liability based on your annual NET income (income less expenses) for the year. The Annual Budget and Bill Tracking Worksheet (See Chapter 3--Section Two) automatically calculates the amount of income that should be put in savings each month toward the tax deposits. When you move funds from checking to savings, do a General Journal entry to show the transfer and then log the transfer to the Savings Ledger (See Chapter 3--Section Nine and Chapter 4--Section Three).

When you are ready to make each of your first three quarterly deposits, use the Annual Budget and Bill Tracking Worksheet to determine how much to transfer back from savings into checking and then deposit the necessary funds to the IRS through their E.F.T.P.S. system (See Chapter 3--Section Eleven).

State Tax Deposits

You will need to check with your State for their requirements (if any) of estimated tax deposits and where to deposit them. Again, the funds should have been saved and transferred into your savings account until they are needed.

Recording Tax Deposit Entries

When you make a tax deposit, you will record the tax deposit as a check written to the IRS or your State Revenue Department. The tax deposit is NOT considered a business expense. The 'expense' account to which you will apply the payment is "Owner's Draw."

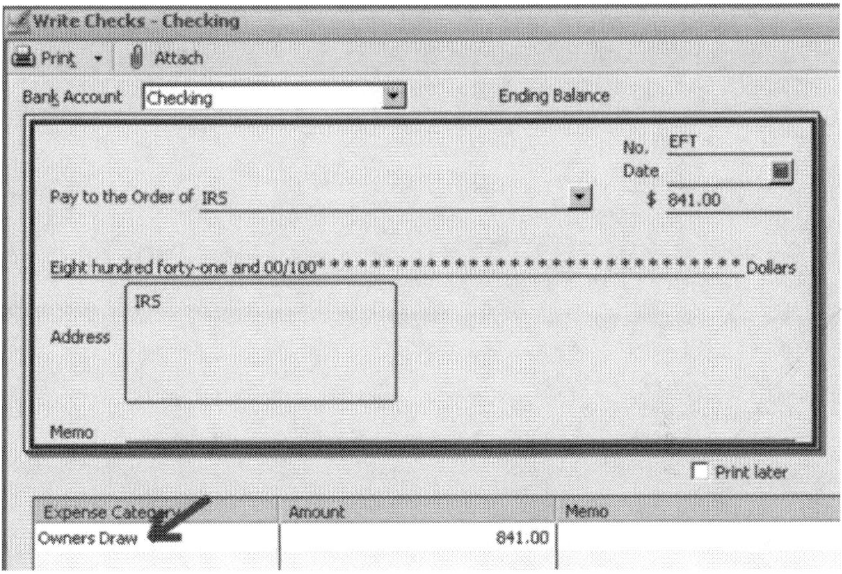

Section Six: Reconciliations in QuickBooks Simple Start

Reconciling Bank Accounts/Loan accounts/Credit Card Accounts

When you receive your bank account/loan statement/credit account statement(s) each month, you should reconcile these statements to your corresponding QuickBooks Simple Start account. Click on Company--For Your Accountant--Reconcile. Click on the dropdown box to choose the account you wish to reconcile (i.e. Checking, Savings, Credit Card).

Enter the Statement Date and Ending Balance from the statement. The Beginning Balance should match the Statement Beginning Balance (if not, click on What if my beginning balance doesn't match my statement?)

If there are service charges or interest on the bank/loan statement, enter them in the appropriate boxes; enter the closing date from the statement in the date boxes. Click the dropdown boxes to select the correct account for the "Expense: Bank Service Charges" or "Income: Interest" account. Click on "Continue."

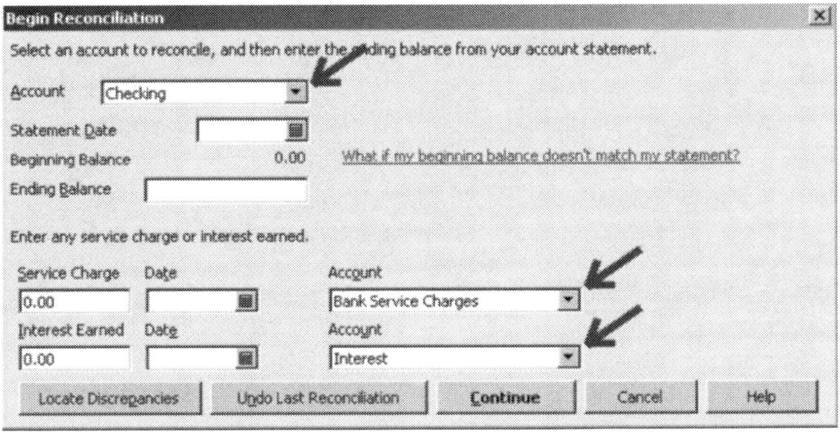

Click on "Hide transactions after the statement's end date" (A). Click on each line item as you match it from the statement; this will place a ✓ next to each "cleared" item (B). When you are done matching the statement to the account items, your "Difference" should be 0.00 (C).

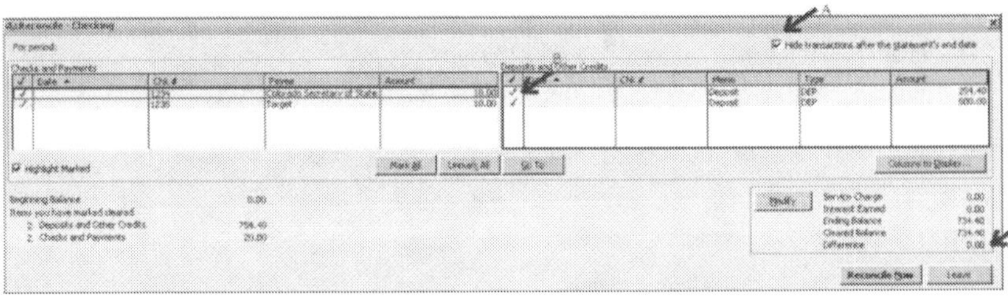

If the difference is NOT 0.00, you will need to find the discrepancy between the items on the statement and the items you cleared. Once you locate the errors or missing items, you will need to either correct or add these items. Click on "Leave." If the error is a deposit or check amount, you will need to go back to the original deposit or check to make the adjustment (Invoices--List or Deposits--List in the left-hand menu). If it is a missing item, simply enter the new item as usual. Return to Company--For Your Accountant-- Reconcile and click on "Continue." Check off the corrected items and verify that the "Difference" is now 0.00.

When you are done reconciling the statement to the account, click on "Reconcile Now." Print both reports to pdf files, print the pdfs onto paper and file them with the reconciled statement in the appropriate physical and electronic files.

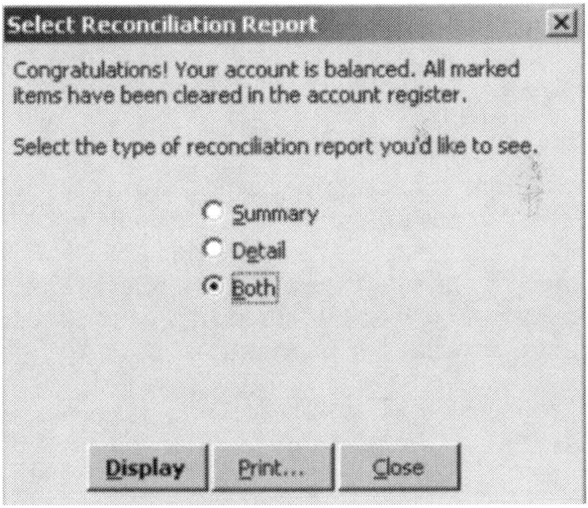

Reconciling Petty Cash

Reconciling Petty Cash/Cash on Hand is the same process but, of course, you won't receive a statement! Simply use your Petty Cash Reconciliation Form to be sure that all entries were made for the month.

Section Seven: Entering Current Fiscal Year Transactions

Now that you understand the process of maintaining your bookkeeping, it is time to begin the process. Start by sorting all of your client, vendor, credit card, etc. records ***by month***.

Starting with the first available month of your current fiscal year business records, enter all of your client records, vendor records, credit card receipts, etc. File the records in your electronic and physical files when the entries are completed.

Once the first month's records are entered, reconcile your bank, loan, credit card, and petty cash accounts.

Now enter the next month's records, followed by reconciling the accounts and then filing the records. Repeat this process until all records are entered up to the current date.

If you have tax deposit(s) due be sure and take care of them now, as well!

Set up a regular schedule for doing your bookkeeping procedures; I recommend paying your bills once/week and scheduling a small amount of time daily to enter your vendor invoices as you receive them. Generating client invoicing/statements will be based on your contract agreements, as will your payment terms.

Chapter 5

Year-end Procedures

Section One: 1099s

IRS regulations require all vendors who were paid over $600 during the prior fiscal year to be issued a 1099 Form by the business who paid them. The IRS then uses this information to verify the amount of income reported on annual tax returns by the vendors. The filing deadlines are as follows:

January 31 – 1099-MISC to subcontractors/vendors
February 28 – Federal 1096/1099-MISC to the IRS.

Issuing 1099 Forms

To determine which vendors to whom *you* need to issue a 1099, run the "Total expenses by payee" report. Click on Reports--Total expenses by payee.

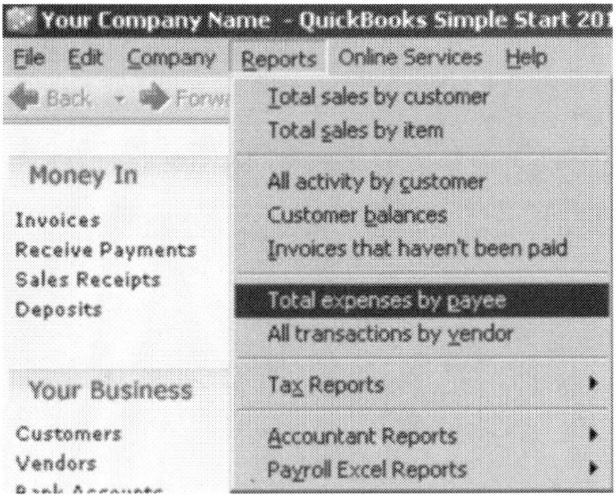

Click on "Modify Report"(A). Change the "Report Date Range" to 'Last Fiscal Year' (B), "Report Basis" to 'Cash' (C), and "Display rows by" to 'Vendor' (D). Click "OK."

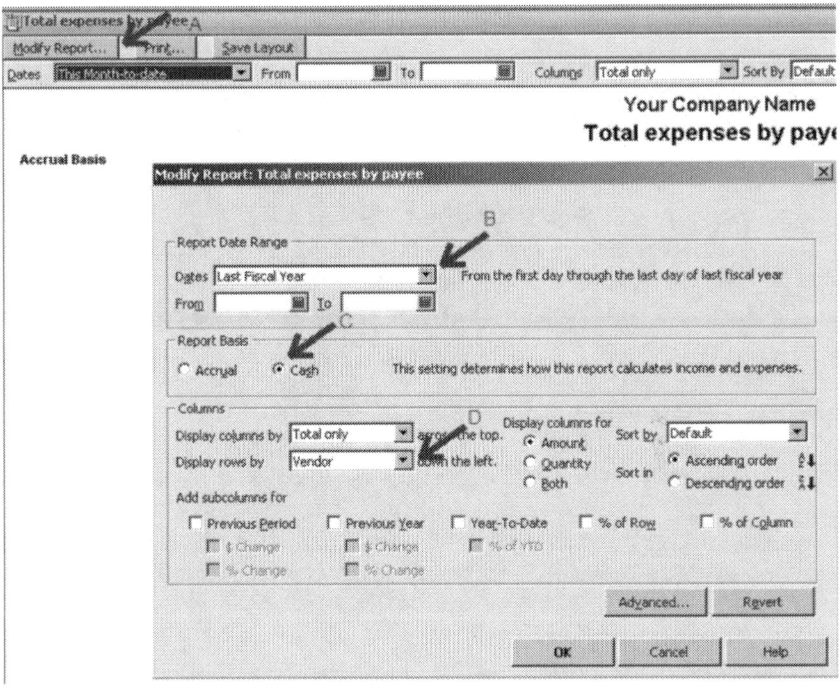

The report will now show all vendors who were paid during the last fiscal year. Go through the list to see which vendors were paid more than $600 and make a note of them. In the report example below, only 'First Vendor" would be issued a 1099 for the prior year.

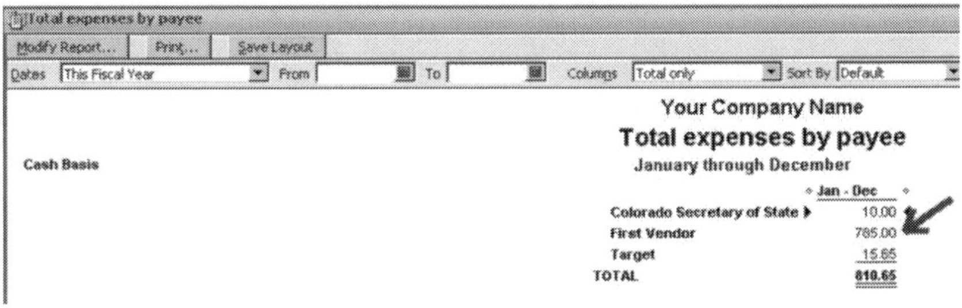

Create the 1099 Forms

Blank 1099 forms are available from your local office supply; they will come with a 1096 Form as well, which is the 'Consolidated Information Form' that gets sent to the

IRS with all 1099 copies. Look for a 1099 forms package that comes with software for completing the forms. Use the software provided with the blank 1099 forms to create the necessary 1099/1096 forms. The copies are filed as follows:

Copy A – IRS (with 1096 form)
Copy 1 – State Revenue Dept
Copy 2 – Recipient (vendor)
Copy B – Recipient (vendor for their state taxes)
Copy C – Payer (Issuer of 1099)

What To Do With Received 1099 Forms

You probably won't receive 1099 forms from all of your clients. However, when you do receive a 1099 Form from a client, verify the amount on the form against what you were actually paid; let the client know if there is a discrepancy so they can issue you (and the IRS) a corrected 1099. Keep all received 1099s in a manila file for future reference.

Section Two: Making Fourth Quarter Tax Deposits for The Prior Fiscal Year

The fourth quarter income/self employment tax deposits of the "fiscal year" are due no later than January 15 of the following year. To verify your previous year's *net* income (income less expenses) you can run a "Profit and Loss" report. Click on Profit & Loss--View in the left-hand menu, or click on the "Profit & Loss" icon.

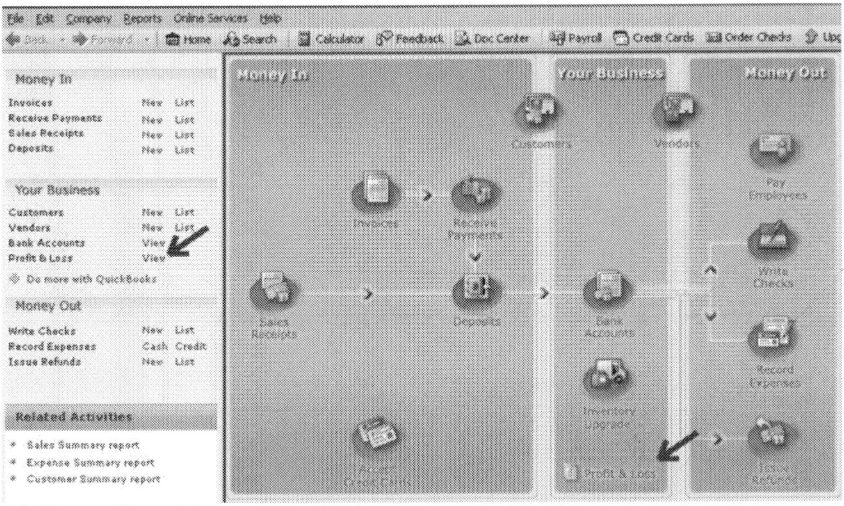

Click on "Modify Report"(A). Change the "Report Date Range" to 'Last Fiscal Year'(B), and "Report Basis" to 'Cash'(C).

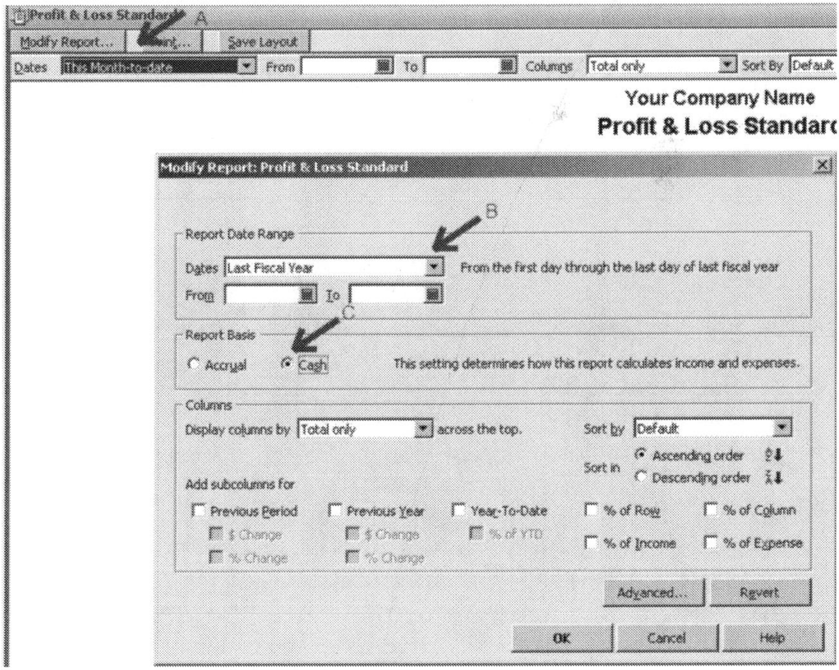

The Profit & Loss (P&L) report will now show you your net income for the previous year, allowing you to calculate your final tax deposits more accurately. In addition, if you have adjusted the actual income in the Annual Budget & Billing Worksheet, the final year-end deposit will have been calculated for you.

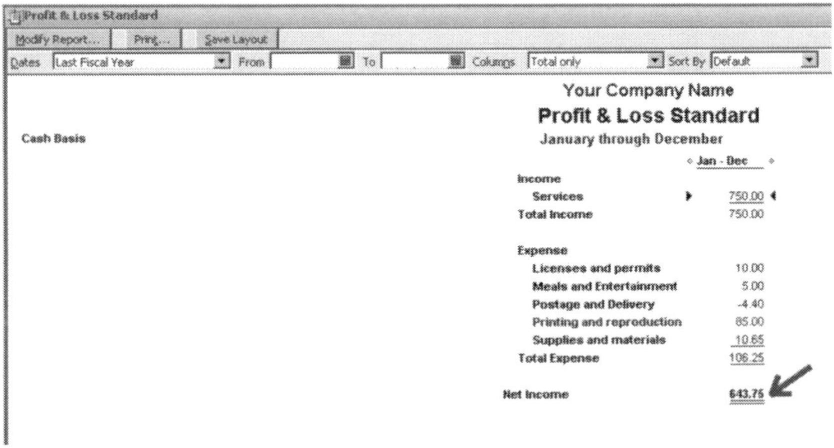

Once you know your prior year's net income, you can calculate the amount of the final quarterly Federal income tax deposit by multiplying your Net Income x 18% and subtracting the dollar amount of the deposits you made during the prior year and deposit the balance due.

Example:

Net Income x 18%	$116	(643.75 x 18%)
Less deposit 04/15	24	
Less deposit 07/15	33	
Less deposit 09/15	35	
To be deposited 01/15	$ 24	

You will calculate your fourth quarter self-employment tax deposit by multiplying your estimated annual net income by 0.9235 (92.35%). (If this amount is less than $400, you don't have to pay self-employment tax.) Now multiply the amount of your net earnings up to $76,200 by 0.153 (15.3%), and multiply any net earnings over $76,200 by

0.029 (2.9%). Add your two numbers together. This is your estimated annual self-employment tax. (This amount is automatically calculated on the Annual Budget & Billing Worksheet.) Next subtract the dollar amount of the deposits you made during the prior year and deposit the balance due.

Section Three: Small Business Deductions To Track For Your Accountant

1. Auto Expenses
2. Expenses of Going into Business
3. Education Expenses
4. Legal and Professional Fees
5. Bad Debts
6. Business Entertainment
7. Travel
8. New Equipment
9. Interest
10. Moving Expenses
11. Software
12. Charitable Contributions
13. Taxes
14. Advertising and Promotion
    - audio and videotapes related to business skills
    - bank service charges
    - business association dues
    - business gifts
    - business-related magazines and books
    - casual labor and tips
    - casualty and theft losses
    - coffee and beverage service
    - commissions
    - consultant fees
    - credit bureau fees
    - office supplies
    - online computer services related to business
    - parking and meters
    - petty cash funds
    - postage
    - promotion and publicity
    - seminars and trade shows
    - taxi and bus fare
    - telephone calls away from the business

Section Four: Providing Records To Your Accountant

Intuit (makers of QuickBooks Simple Start) has made a simple program to help get your tax information to your accountant at year end. The first step is to create a "Portable company file." Click on File--Save Copy or Backup" (A). Then click on "Portable Company File" (B) and click "Finish" (C).

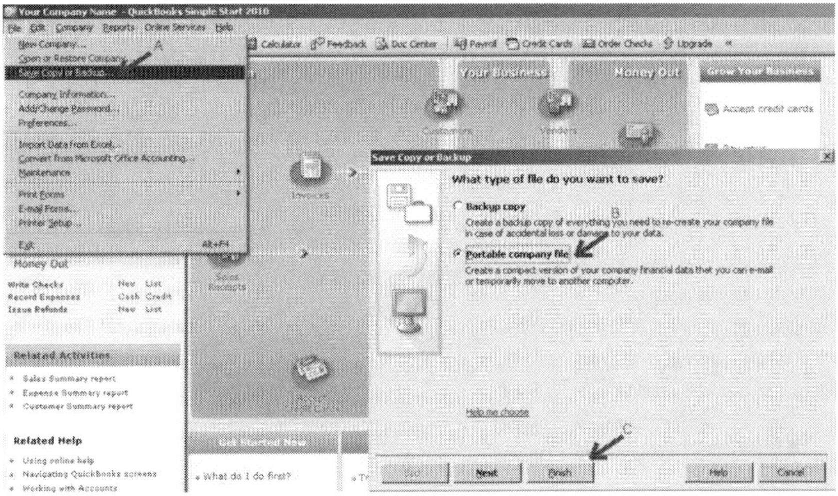

You have now created a .qbm file that can then be sent to your accountant.

Install the QuickBooks File Transfer Tool (http://support.quickbooks.intuit.com/support/pages/contentsections/pages/SimpleStartFileTransfer). Run the File Transfer program, click on "Upload a file" then click "Next." Now click on "Browse", locate the .qbm file that you created, and click on "Next."

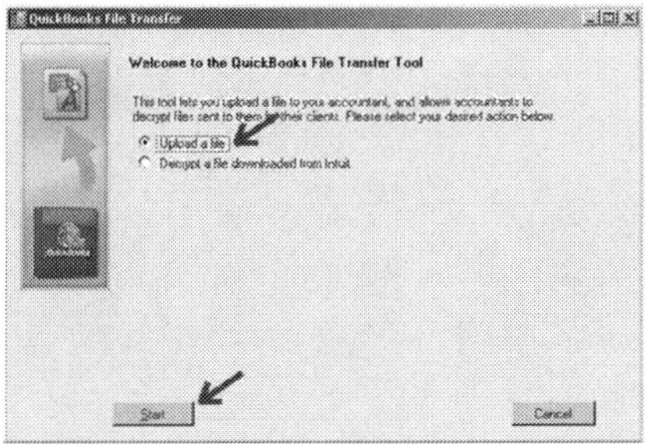

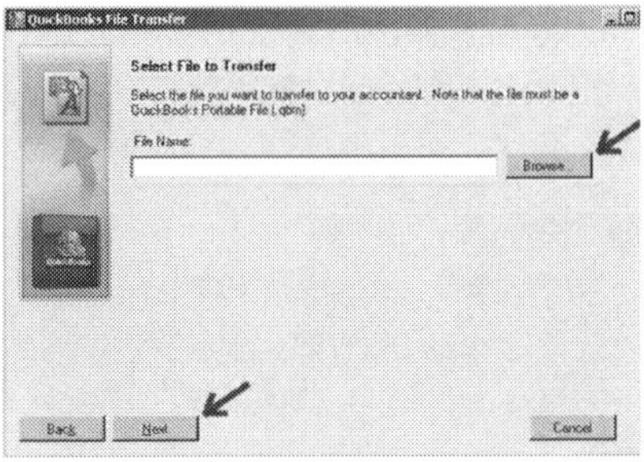

Fill in the "Accountant's email address", "Reenter accountant's email address", "Your name" and "Your email address" boxes and click "Next." Now fill in the "Create file transfer password to encrypt file for security", "Reenter password", and "Note to your accountant" (if you have any notes) boxes and click on "Submit."

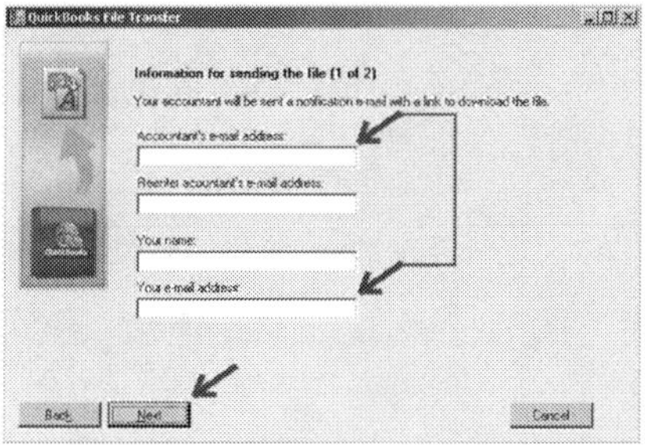

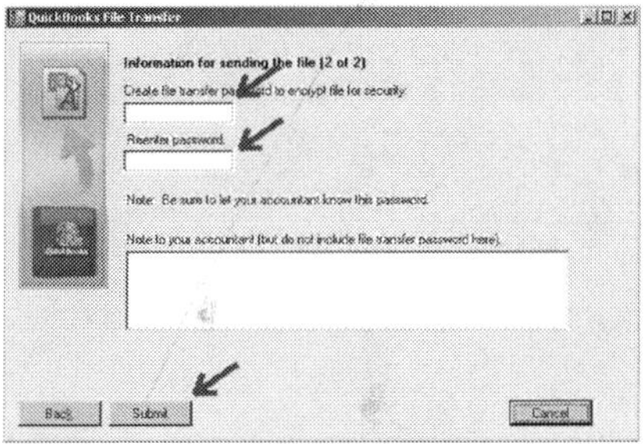

Be sure and contact your accountant with the password! For good security, your password should be a minimum of eight characters, contain both upper and lower-case alpha-numeric characters and include a non-alpha-numeric character (e.g. Books2U!).

Section Five: Closing Out Your End-of-Year QuickBooks Accounts

"Unlike many accounting systems, QuickBooks does not require that books be closed at the end of an accounting period. Because QuickBooks does not formally close out any accounting period, transactions can be entered for any time period. One reason for closing the books in QuickBooks is to restrict access to the transactions of prior accounting periods, so that transactions cannot be changed" (from QuickBooks website)

QuickBooks Simple Start does NOT have an easy way to 'close out' your books in order to separate time periods. Therefore, you will need to make the necessary General Journal entries to 'clean up' your income/expense files and 'start fresh' for the new year.

The Income and Expense accounts need to be zeroed out for the year. First, the income accounts balances are moved to the "Income Summary" account:

Date	**Accounts**	**Debit**	**Credit**
12/31	*"Income Account(s)"*	X	
	Income Summary		X

Now, the expense accounts balances are moved to the "Income Summary" account:

Date	**Accounts**	**Debit**	**Credit**
12/31	Income Summary	X	
	"Expense Accounts"		X

And finally, the "Income Summary" account balance is moved to "Retained Earnings."

Date	**Accounts**	**Debit**	**Credit**
12/31	Retained Earnings	X	
	Income Summary		X

To determine what numbers to use, run a Profit and Loss report (See Chapter 5--SectionTwo) and use it to make the General Journal entries (example below).

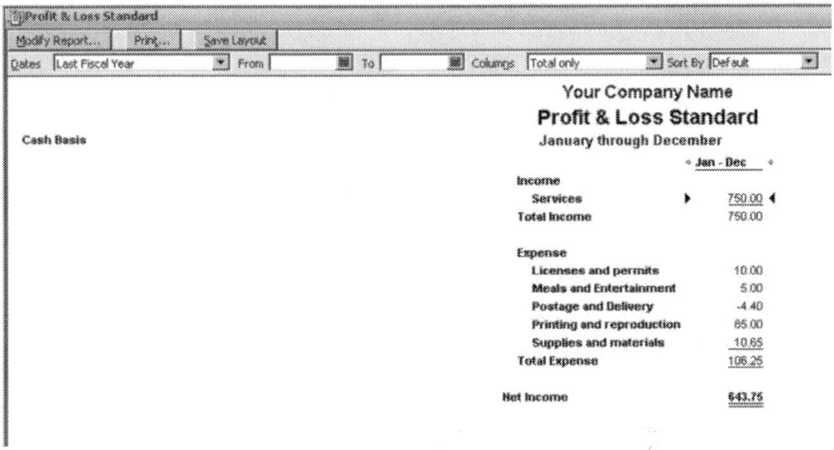

The "Total Income" listed in the above example is $750.00 . Therefore, your general journal entry would look like this:

Date	Accounts	Debit	Credit
12/31	Services (income)	750.00	
	Income Summary		750.00

The "Total Expense" listed is $106.25

Date	Accounts	Debit	Credit
12/31	Income Summary	106.25	
	Licenses and permits		10.00
	Meals and Entertainment		5.00
	Postage and Delivery	4.40	
	Printing and reproduction		85.00
	Supplies and materials		10.65

The "Net Income" listed is $643.75

Date	Accounts	Debit	Credit
12/31	Retained Earnings	643.75	
	Income Summary		643.75

When you are done making your entries, open the Chart of Accounts (CTRL-A) and verify that the "Income Summary Account" is zero.

Although you CAN make all of the entries in one General Journal entry, do it as three separate entries to make it less confusing.

Section Six: Archiving Files

Physical Files

Physical files can be placed into an unused filing cabinet drawer, a 'bankers box', or an expanding folder. Mark the 'archival container' with the appropriate date (e.g. Accounting files 20..) and then make a new set of 'blank' folders for the new year's files.

Electronic Files

Electronic files can be transferred into an 'archived' folder on the computer (name the folder "Accounting files [YEAR]) if you wish to have quick access to them. I also recommend burning the files onto a blank cd-rom and placing that with the archived physical files. Again, make a new set of electronic folders for the new year's files.

Chapter 6

Final Exam

FINAL EXAM - Bookkeeping for Virtual Assistants & Entrepreneurs

I recommend 'taking' the final exam just as a way to reinforce what you have learned! The answers are in the next chapter so you can double-check that you understand the information.

QUESTION	ANSWER A	ANSWER B	ANSWER C
1. In *accounting* terms, how do "credits" and "debits" affect your bank account? Answer_____	A credit decreases the account A debit increases the amount	They don't affect my bank account	A credit increases the amount A debit decreases the amount
2. Why is a budget important? Answer _____	You will need a budget to apply for a bank loan.	It makes your business seem more professional.	To help you keep track of whether or not your business is making a profit.
3. When are estimated Federal tax deposits due? Answer_____	April 15, July 15, October 15, January 15	April 15, July 15, September 15, January 15	March 31, June 30, September 30, December 31
4. What are three things your timesheet will help you to do? Answer_____	Keep you on track Verify the time worked to a client Prove your honesty	Keep you focused on your work Track your sick days Help you account for your time	Bill your clients Calculate future project time estimates Estimate future income
5. What basic information do you need to build a budget? Answer_____	List of income and expenses	List of current jobs and hours worked on them	List of current clients and vendors

QUESTION	ANSWER A	ANSWER B	ANSWER C
6. What type of accounts should be the most common in your Chart of Accounts? Answer_____	Income	Expense	Miscellaneous
7. What form(s) do you need to set up your bank/credit card/loan accounts in QuickBooks Simple Start? Answer_____	Account statements	Account receipts	List of accounts
8. What are "Items" used for in QuickBooks Simple Start? Answer_____	To track clients	To track vendors	To track income/expense items
9. What types of "items" should be set up? Answer_____	Vendors	Fees and expenses	Clients
10. What is the function of a General Journal entry? Answer_____	To track client payments	To transfer balances between accounts	To track vendor payments
11. What is the function of a petty cash fund? Answer_____	To pay for small expenses instead of writing a check or using a credit card.	To pay your daily latte expense	To pay for parking, tolls, etc.

QUESTION	ANSWER A	ANSWER B	ANSWER C
12. What percentage of your estimated annual net income should you deposit for Federal self-employment tax? Answer_____	25%	18%	10%
13. What percentage of your estimated annual net income should you save for State self-employment tax? Answer_____	15%	10%	7%
14. What type of form do you use to record client deposits in QuickBooks Simple Start? Answer_____	Invoice	Sales Receipt	Deposit Reconciliation form
15. What account do you use to track client deposit funds? Answer_____	Retainer account	Savings account	Checking account
16. Why should you keep receipts for all purchases? Answer_____	To return unwanted items	You will need these if your tax return is audited by the IRS	To track your expenses
17. What information should you write on your purchase receipts? Answer_____	What the receipt is for (supplies, marketing, etc.) and what job it is for (if applicable)	Date, vendor, price	Item description

QUESTION	ANSWER A	ANSWER B	ANSWER C
18. Where does QuickBooks Simple Start track unpaid bills? Answer_____	In the vendor list	In the expenses list of your Profit & Loss report	"To Print" is in the 'number type' column of your checking account
19. How do unpaid bills that are entered affect your check register? Answer_____	They don't affect it	They decrease the available balance	They show up as a separate line item
20. What accounts should be reconciled each month? Answer_____	Bank, credit card, loan, petty cash	Bank, credit card, client, vendor	Bank, loan, petty cash, vendor

Chapter 7

Answers to Research Project and Final Exam

RESEARCH PROJECT ANSWERS

IRS Website (www.irs.gov)

1.	What ID number should you use for your business in place of your Social Security number?	EIN (a TIN is for individuals, not businesses)
2.	What publication number is the "A Virtual Small Business Tax Workshop" DVD?	Publication 1066C
3.	What publication number is the "Tax Calendar for Small Businesses and Self-employed?"	Publication 1518
4.	What is the definition of "Burden of Proof"	The responsibility to prove entries, deductions, and statements made on your tax returns.
5.	How long should you keep your tax records under normal circumstances?	3 years
6. 7. 8.	"To be deductible, a business expense must be both ordinary and necessary." What is the definition of an 'ordinary' expense? What is the definition of a 'necessary' expense?	a) An ordinary expense is one that is common and accepted in your trade or business. b) A necessary expense is one that is helpful and appropriate for your trade or business.
9.	What types of expenses can you deduct for the 'business use of your home?'	Mortgage interest, insurance, utilities, repairs, and depreciation.

FINAL EXAM ANSWERS

QUESTION	ANSWER A	ANSWER B	ANSWER C
1. In accounting terms, how do "credits" and "debits" affect your bank account? Answer A	A credit decreases the account A debit increases the amount	They don't affect my bank account	A credit increases the amount A debit decreases the amount
2. Why is a budget important? Answer C	You will need a budget to apply for a bank loan.	It makes your business seem more professional.	To help you keep track of whether or not your business is making a profit.
3. When are estimated Federal tax deposits due? Answer B	April 15, July 15, October 15, January 15	April 15, July 15, September 15, January 15	March 31, June 30, September 30, December 31
4. What are three things your timesheet will help you to do? Answer C	Keep you on track Verify the time worked to a client Prove your honesty	Keep you focused on your work Track your sick days Help you account for your time	Bill your clients Calculate future project time estimates Estimate future income
5. What basic information do you need to build a budget? Answer A	List of income and expenses	List of current jobs and hours worked on them	List of current clients and vendors
6. What type of accounts should be the most common in your Chart of Accounts? Answer B	Income	Expense	Miscellaneous

7. What form(s) do you need to set up your bank/credit card/loan accounts in QuickBooks Simple Start? Answer A	Account statements	Account receipts	List of accounts
8. What are 'Items' used for in QuickBooks Simple Start? Answer C	To track clients	To track vendors	To track income/expense items
9. What types of items should be set up? Answer B	Vendors	Fees and expenses	Clients
10. What is the function of a General Journal entry? Answer B	To track client payments	To transfer balances between accounts	To track vendor payments
11. What is the function of a petty cash fund? Answer A	To pay for small expenses instead of writing a check or using a credit card.	To pay your daily latte expense	To pay for parking, tolls, etc.
12. What percentage of your estimated annual net income should you deposit for Federal self-employment tax? Answer B	25%	18%	10%

13. What percentage of your estimated annual net income should you save for State self-employment tax? Answer C	15%	10%	7%
14. What type of form do you use to record client deposits in QuickBooks Simple Start? Answer B	Invoice	Sales Receipt	Deposit Reconciliation form
15. What account do you use to track client deposit funds? Answer A	Retainer account	Savings account	Checking account
16. Why should you keep receipts for all purchases? Answer B	To return unwanted items	You will need these if your tax return is audited by the IRS	To track your expenses
17. What information should you write on your purchase receipts? Answer A	What the receipt is for (supplies, marketing, etc.) and what job it is for (if applicable)	Date, vendor, price	Item description
18. Where does QuickBooks Simple Start list unpaid bills? Answer C	In the vendor list	In the expenses list of your Profit & Loss report	"To Print" is in the 'number type' column of your checking account

19. How do unpaid bills that are entered affect your check register? Answer B	They don't affect it	They decrease the available balance	They show up as a separate line item
20. What accounts should be reconciled each month? Answer A	Bank, credit card, loan, petty cash	Bank, credit card, client, vendor	Bank, loan, petty cash, vendor

How To Obtain The Referenced Excel Files:

To obtain the Five Excel spreadsheets referenced in this book, go to www.virtualofficegoddess.com/book.html and fill out your email address at the bottom of the page.

About The Author:

Lily E. Chambers, CPS, CQU owns and operates The Virtual Office Goddess, LLC. In addition, she teaches Basic Bookkeeping for Entrepreneurs (QuickBooks Pro version) for the Academy of Virtual Education, is the Publisher/Editor of The Virtual Evolution Magazine, and the Treasurer on the Board of Whole Systems Institute (a Boulder, CO non-profit).

Ms. Chambers has over three decades of bookkeeping, executive secretarial, office management, and office support experience in the criminal justice, legal (criminal and immigration), water engineering, funeral service, property valuation, landscaping, water/oilfield pipe and supply, manufacturing, food service, hospitality, and retail industries.

NOTES

NOTES

NOTES

Made in United States
Orlando, FL
04 November 2026

90201387R10059